Sugar Skull

COLORING BOOK

I0485600

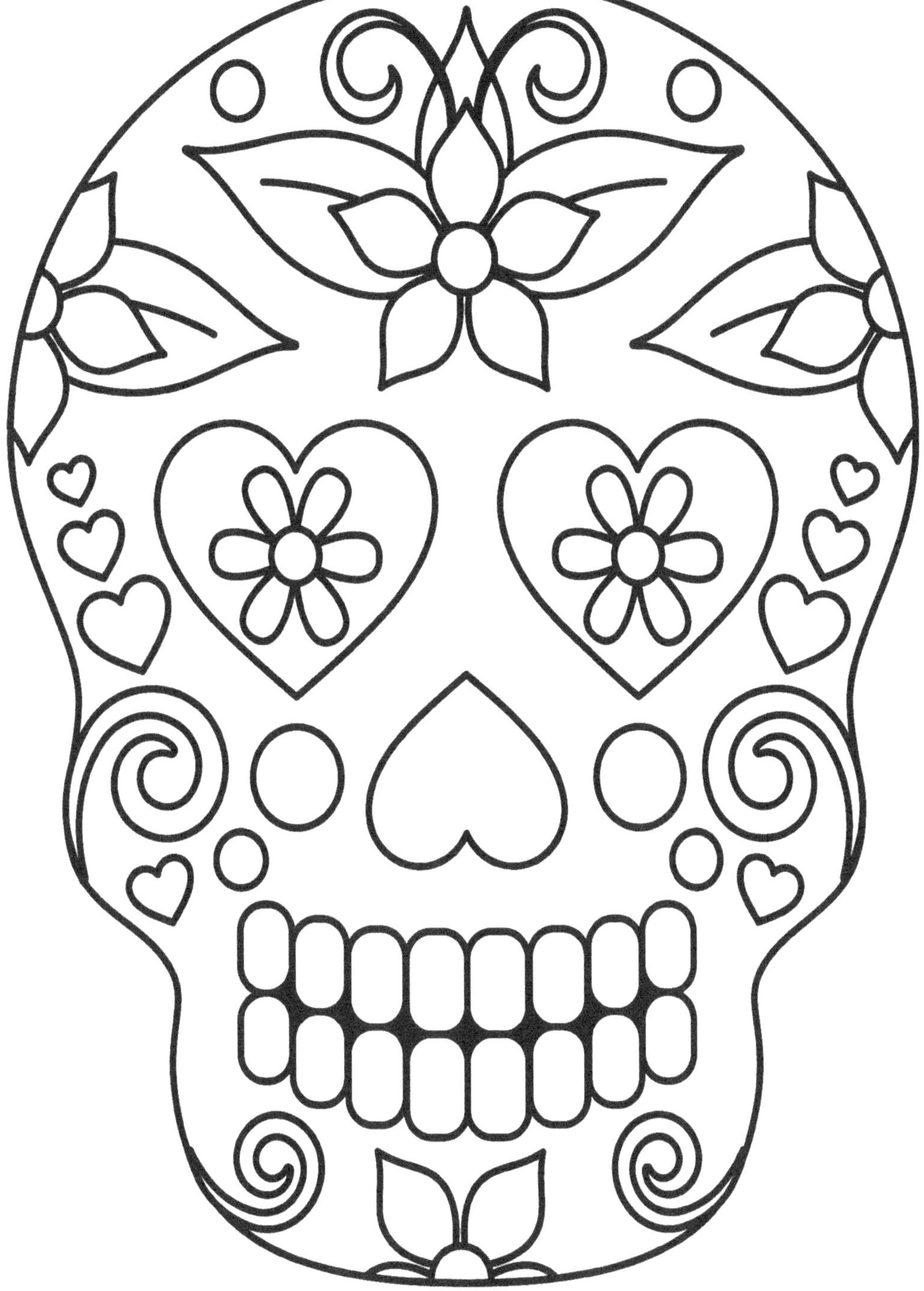

The Book Belongs To:

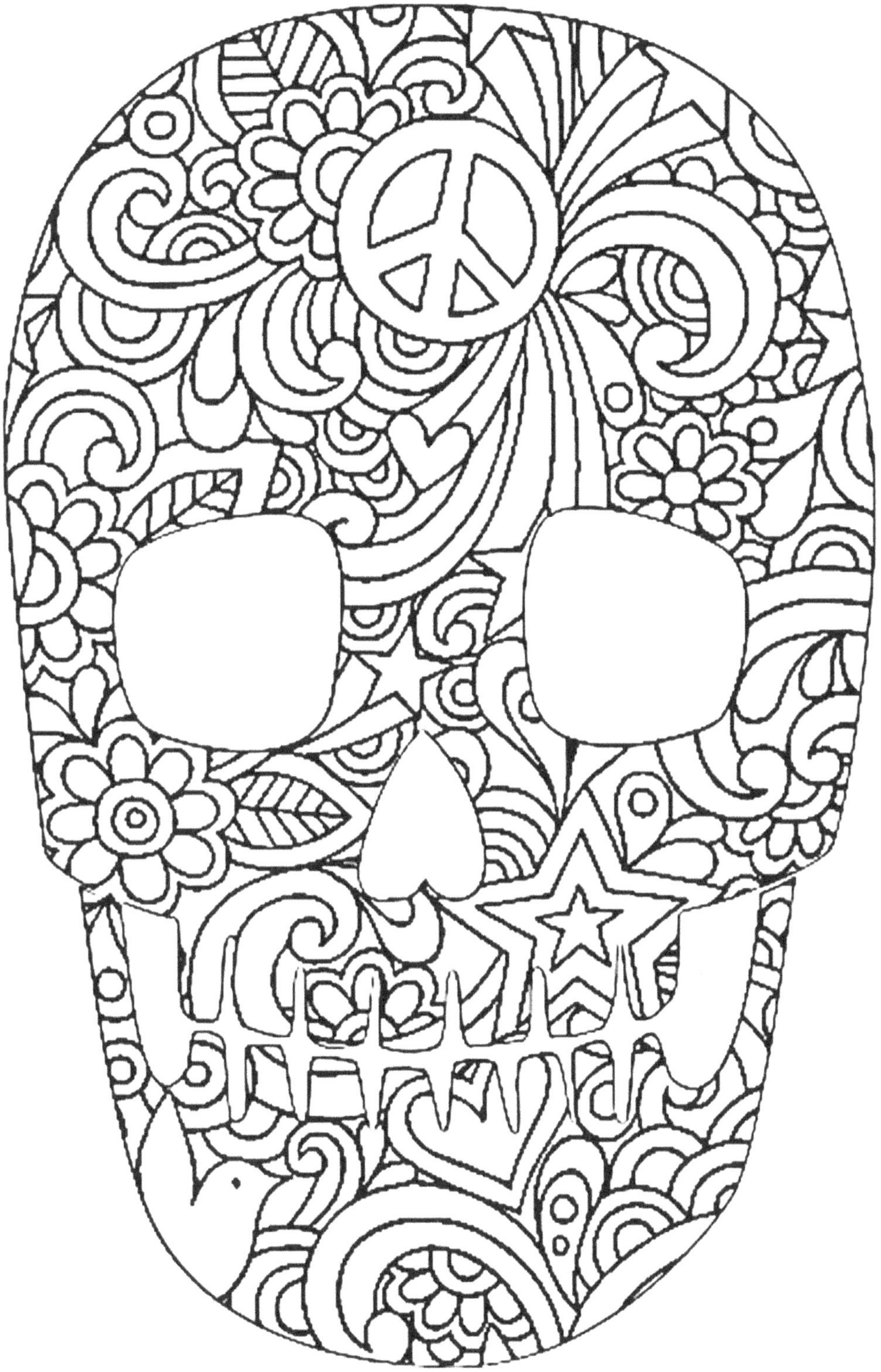

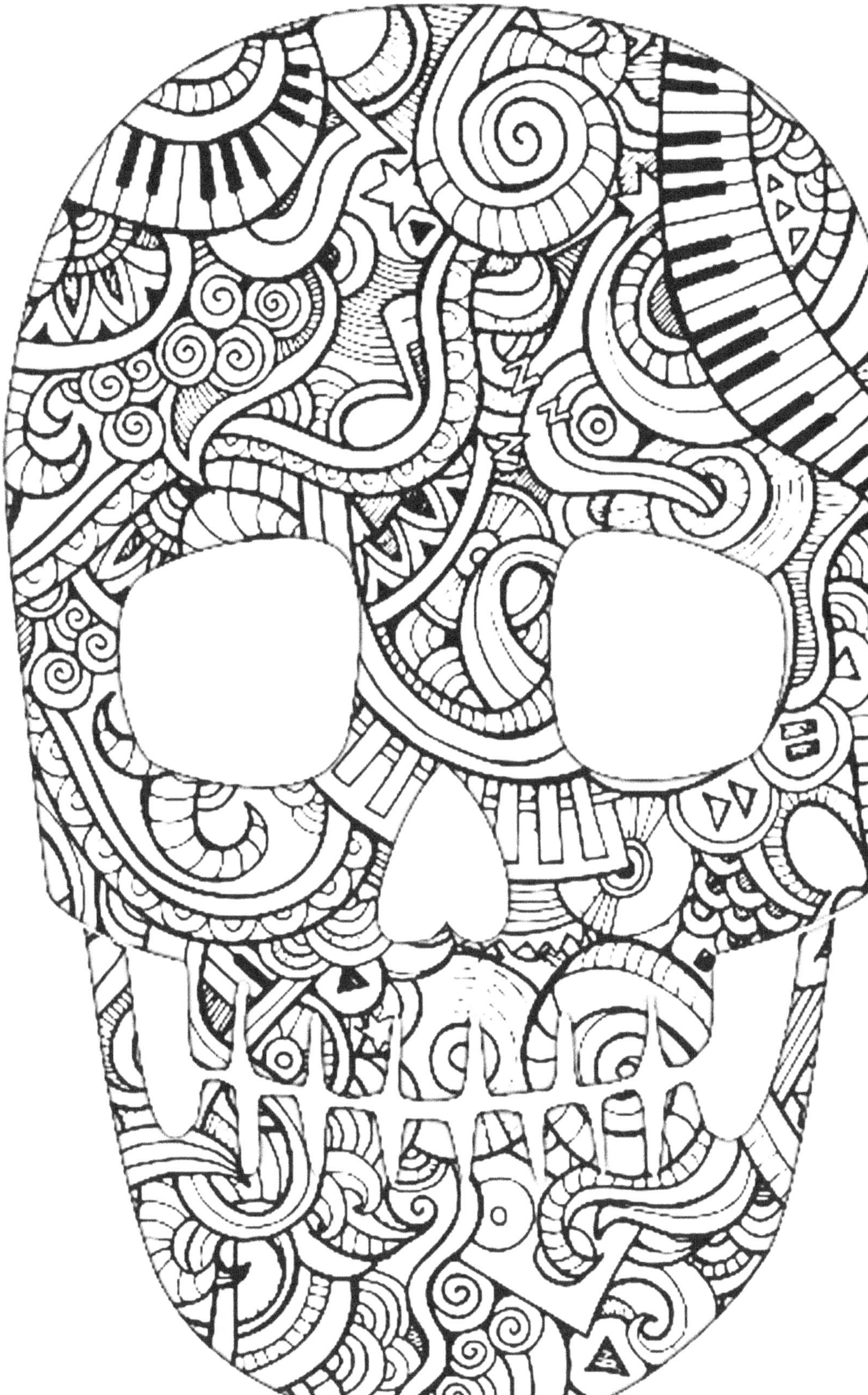

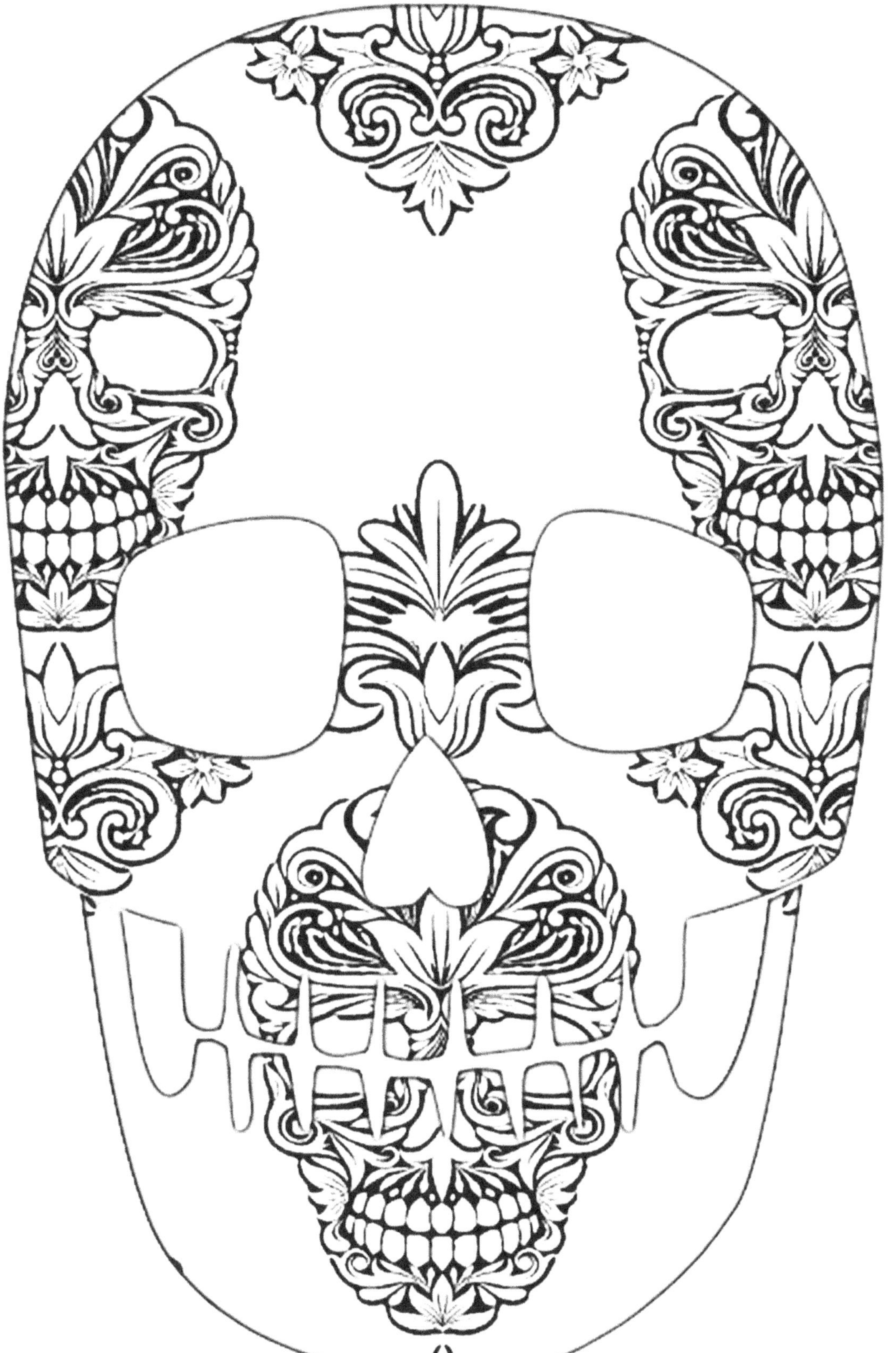

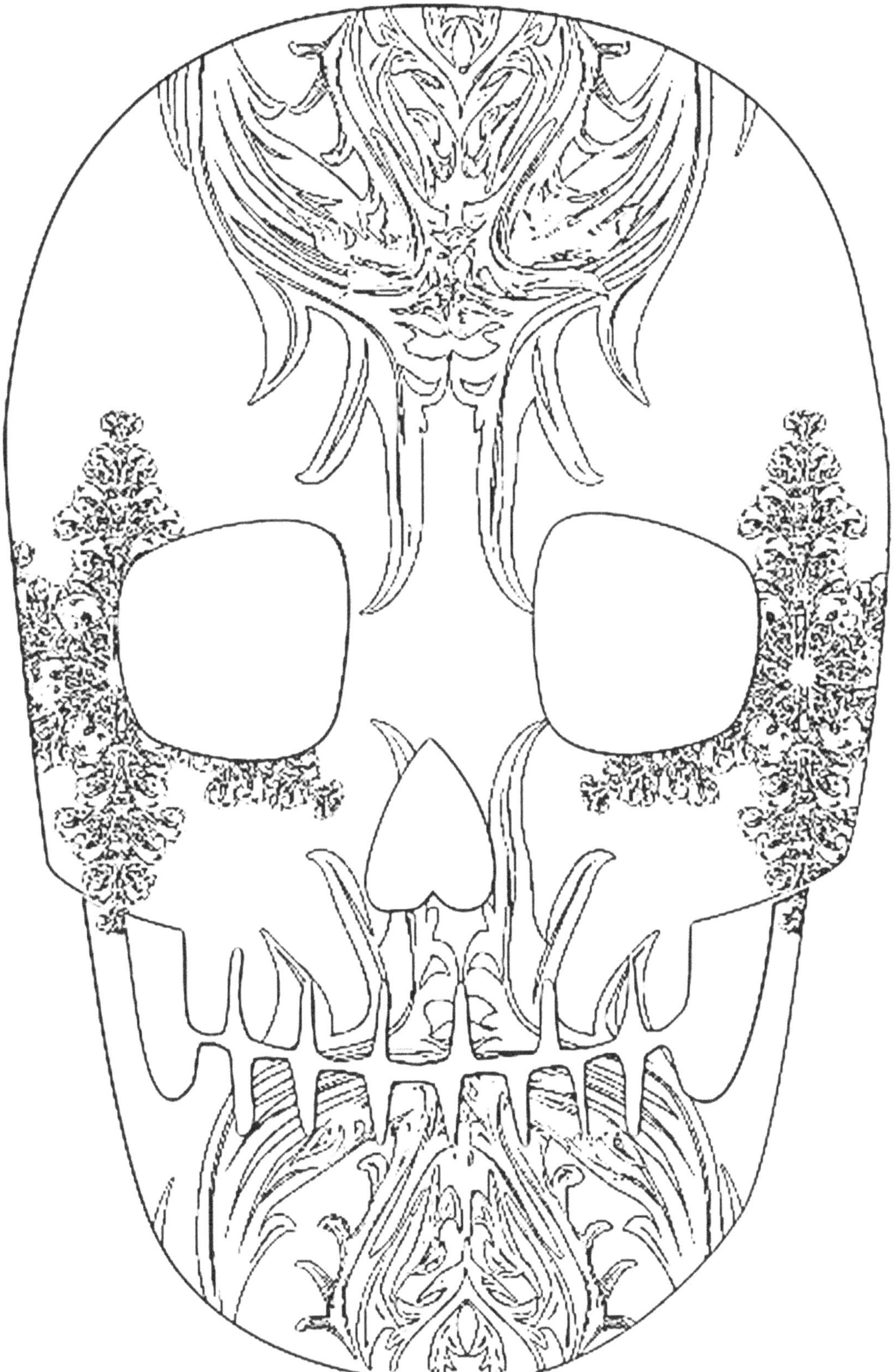

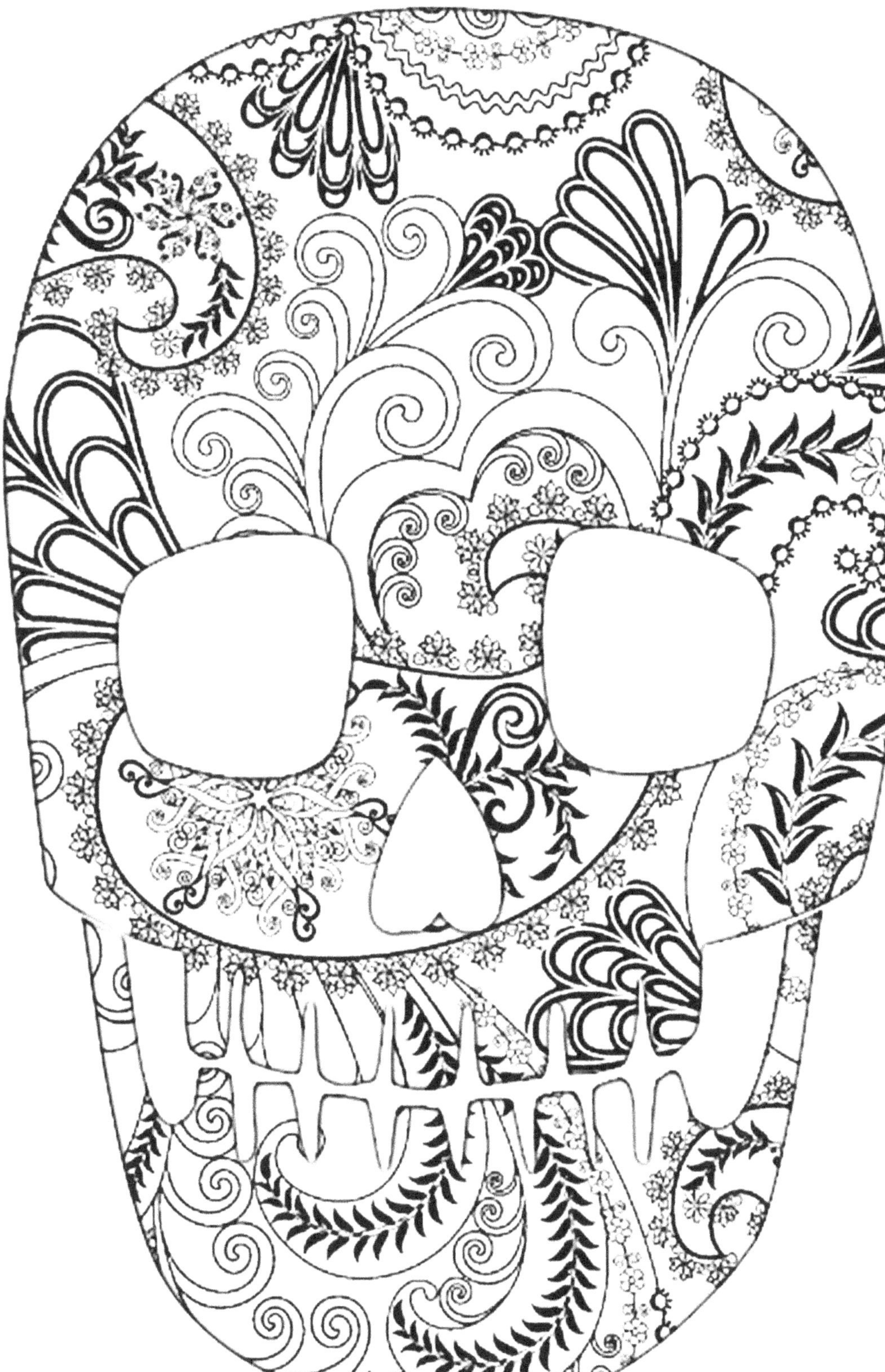

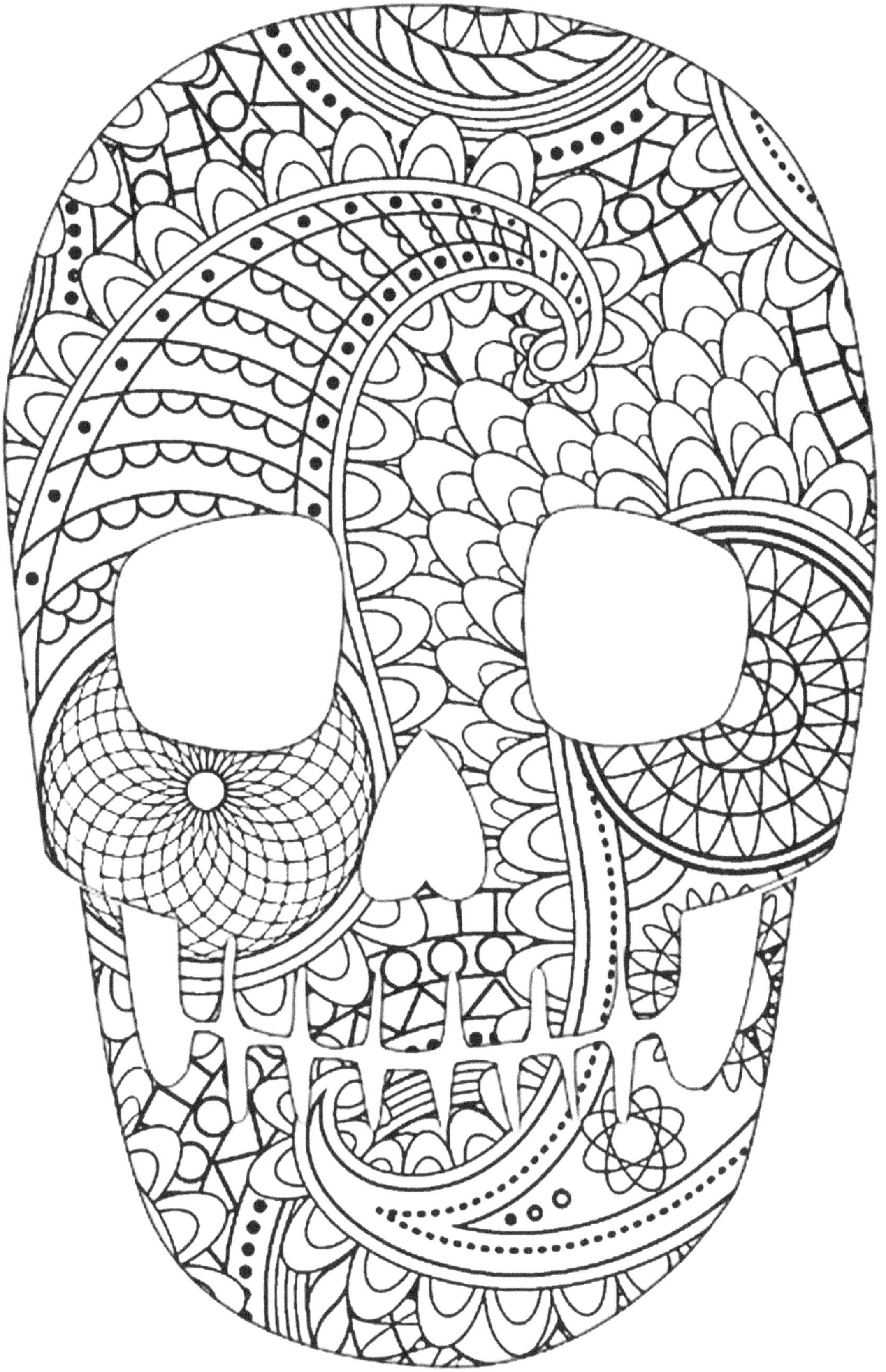

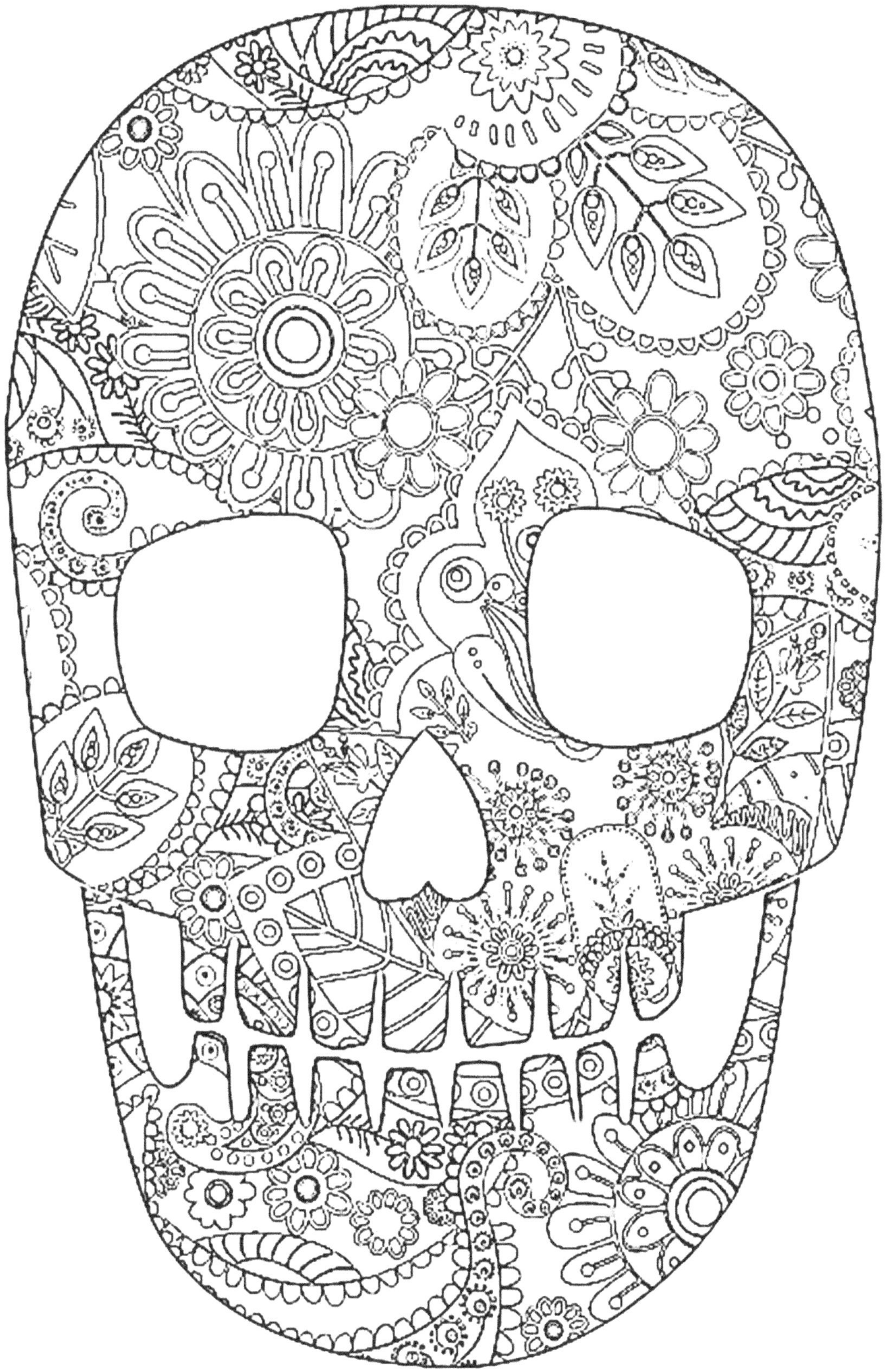

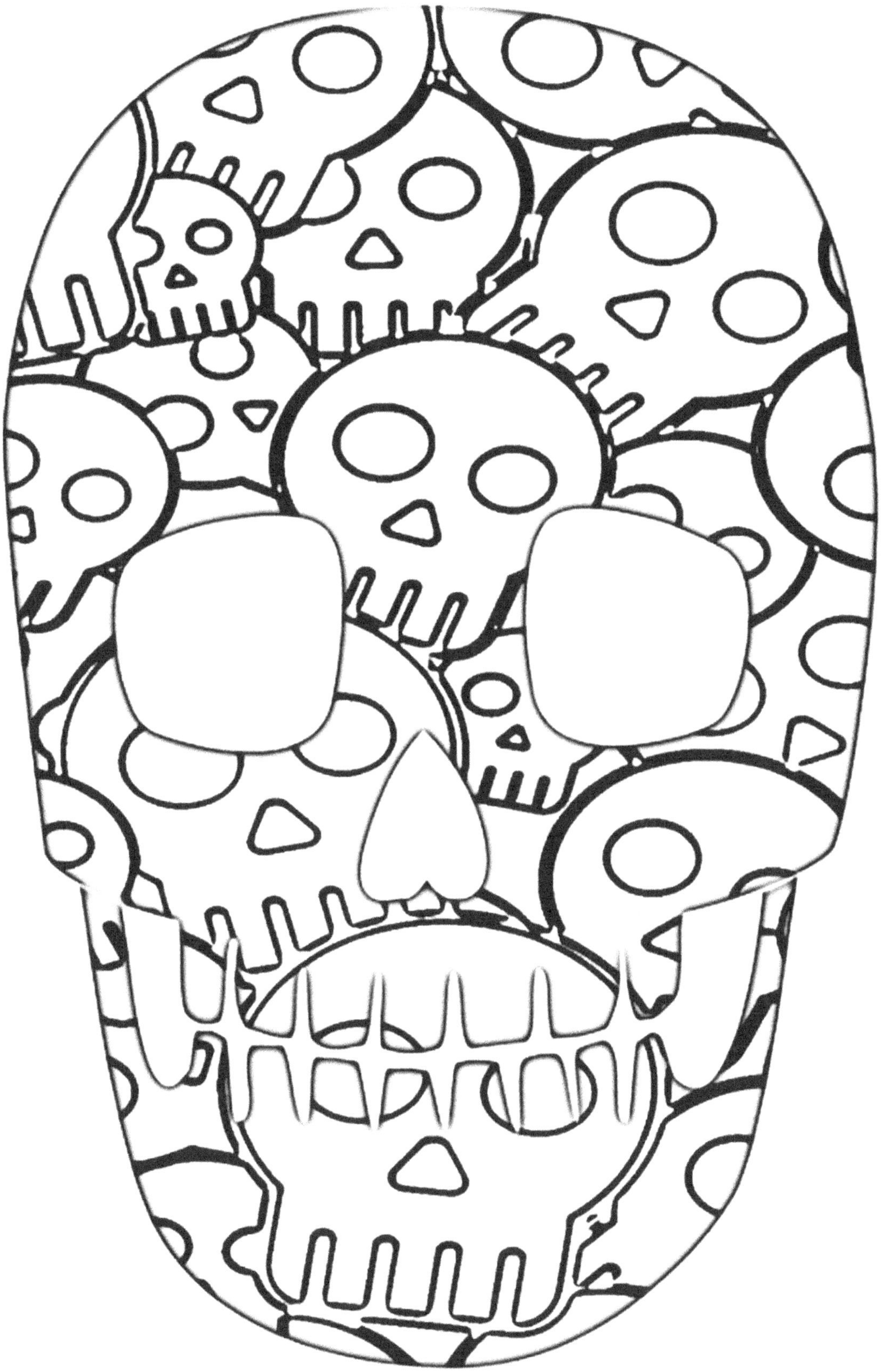

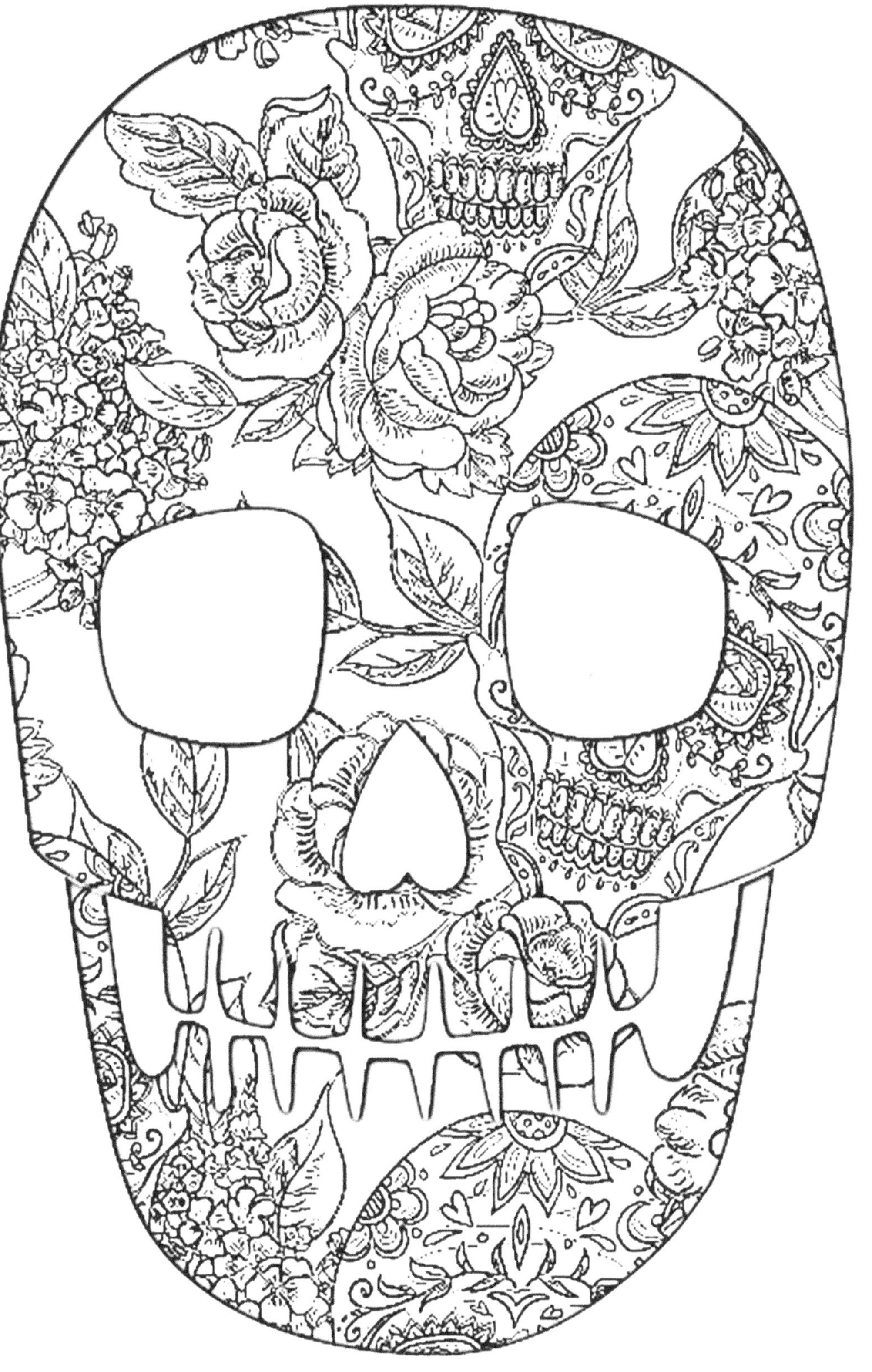

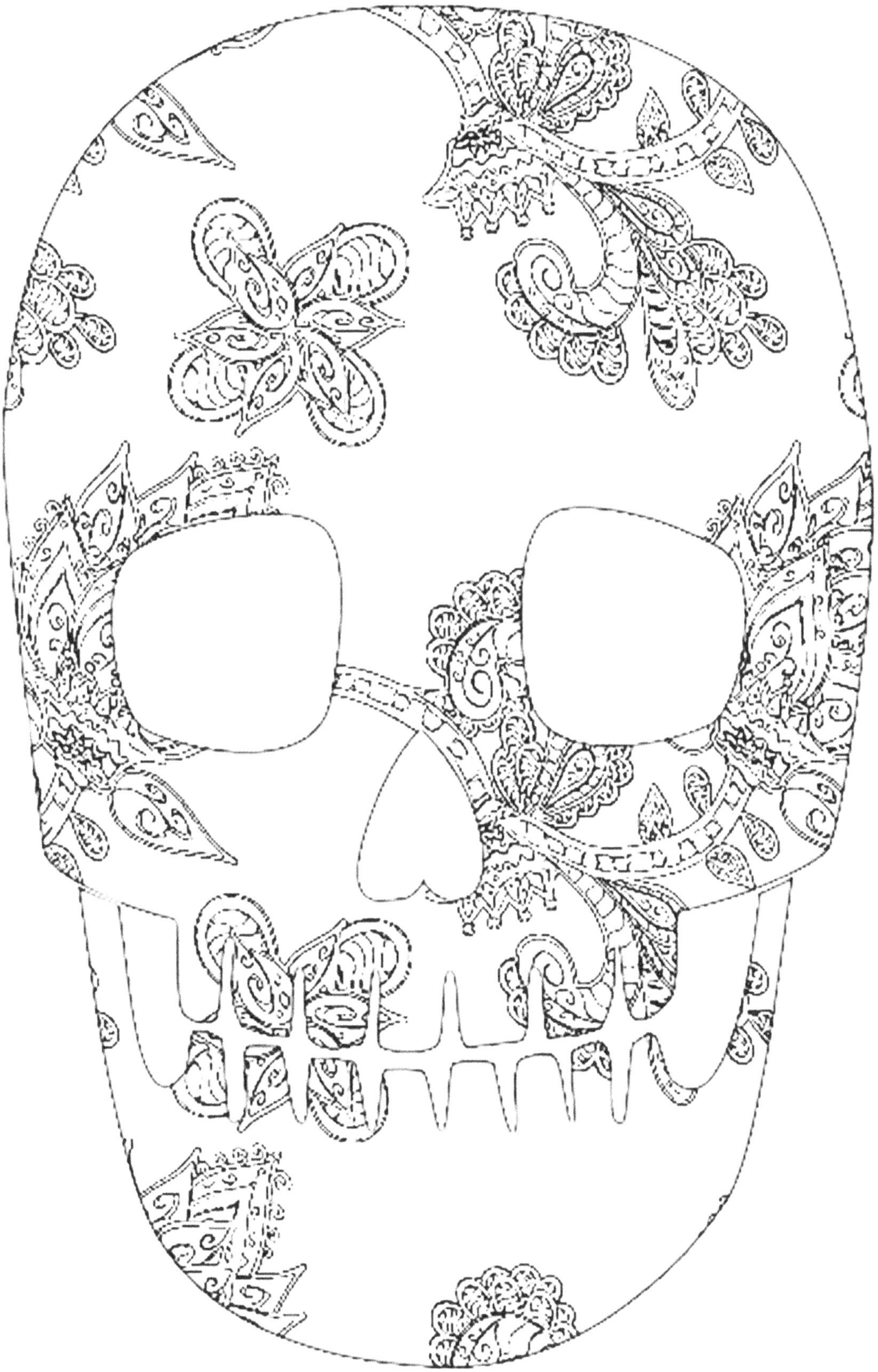

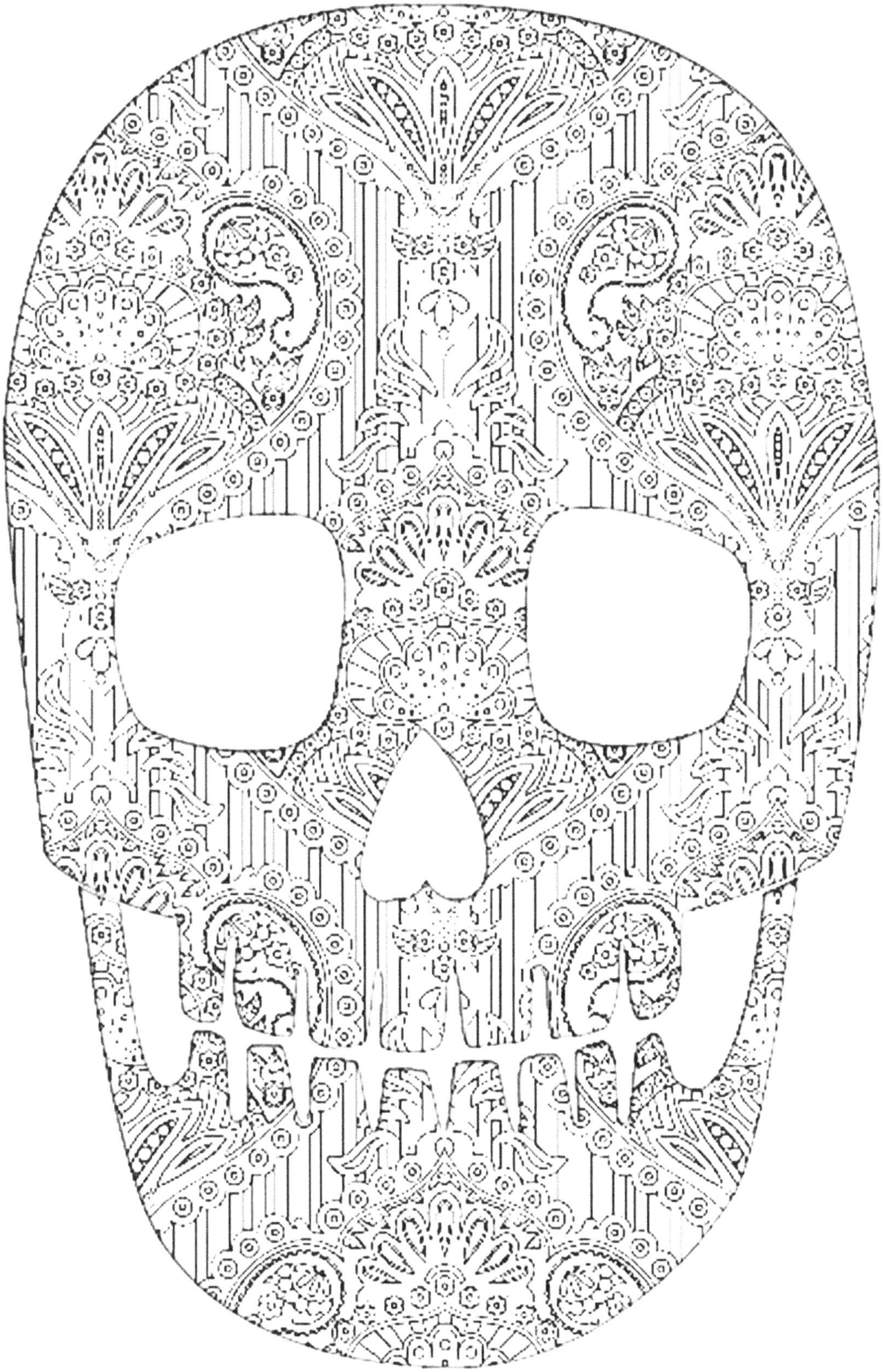

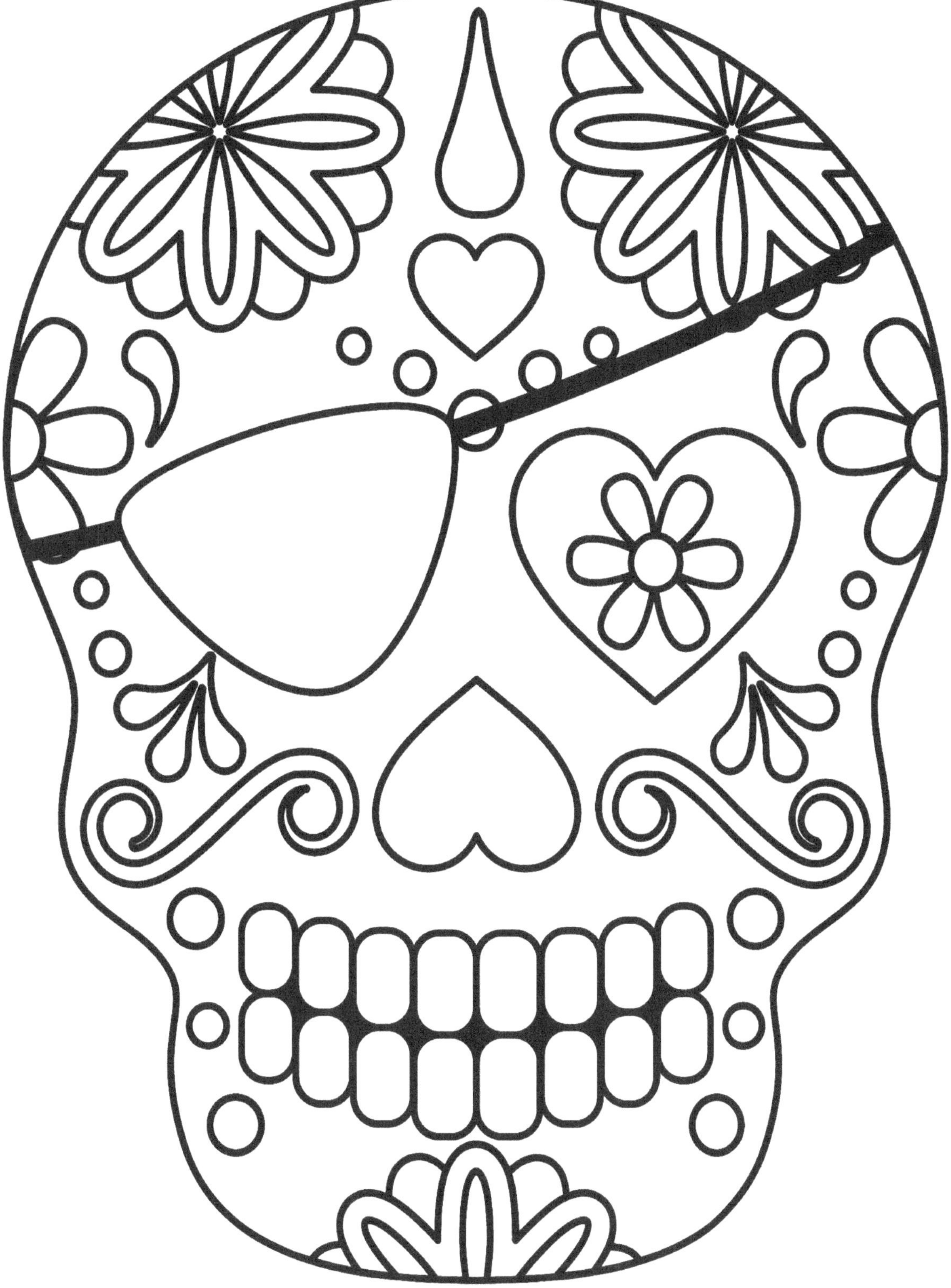

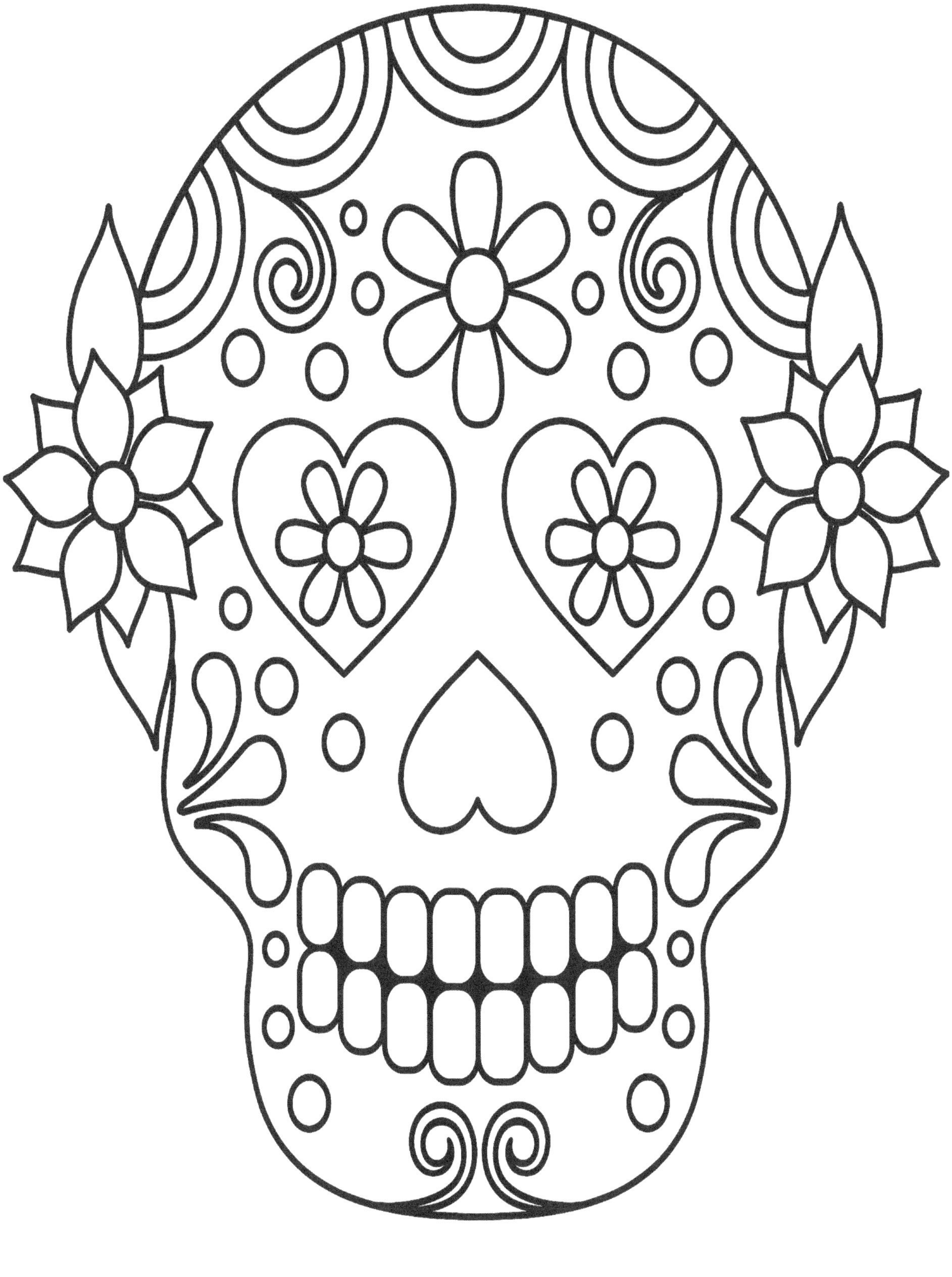

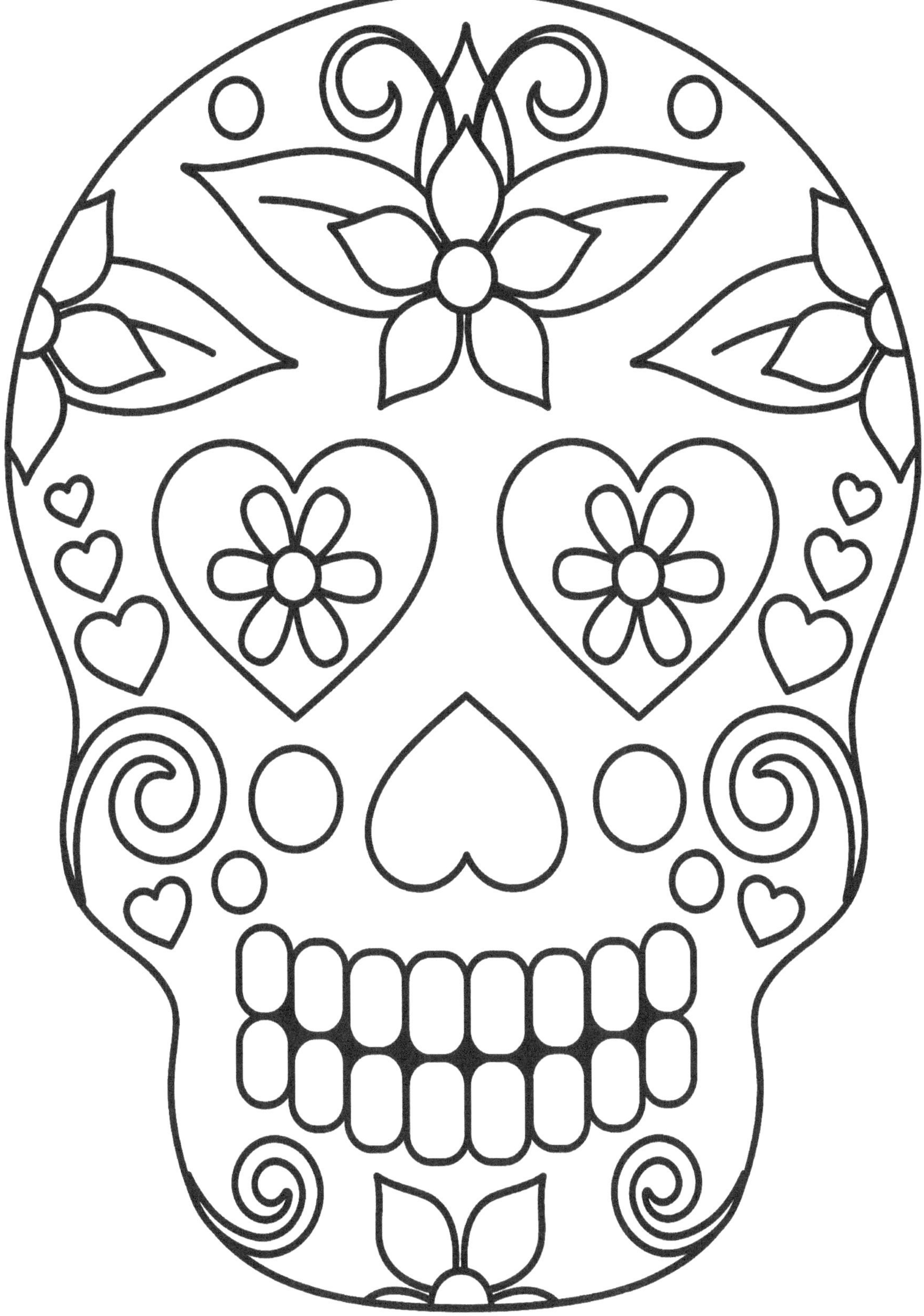

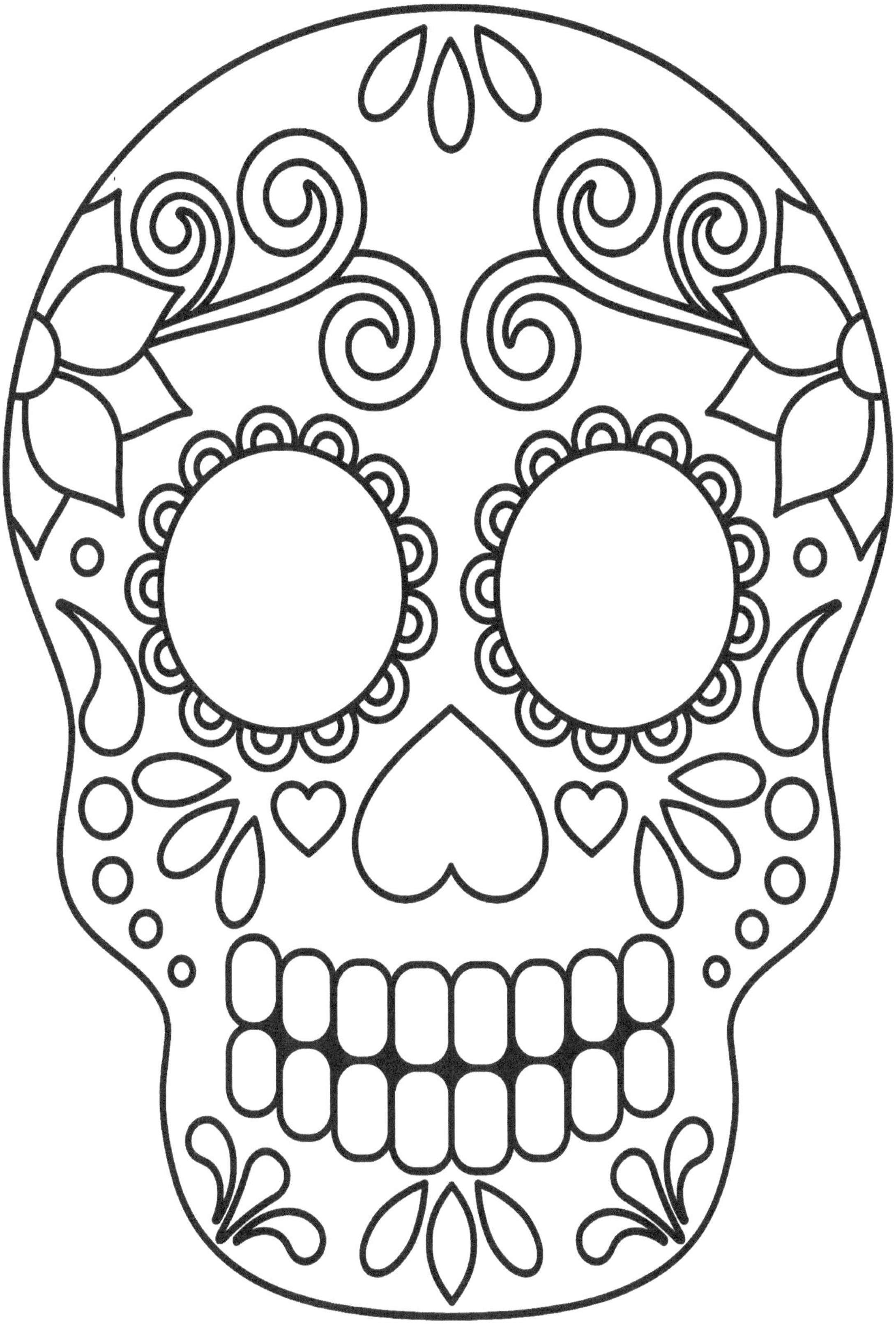

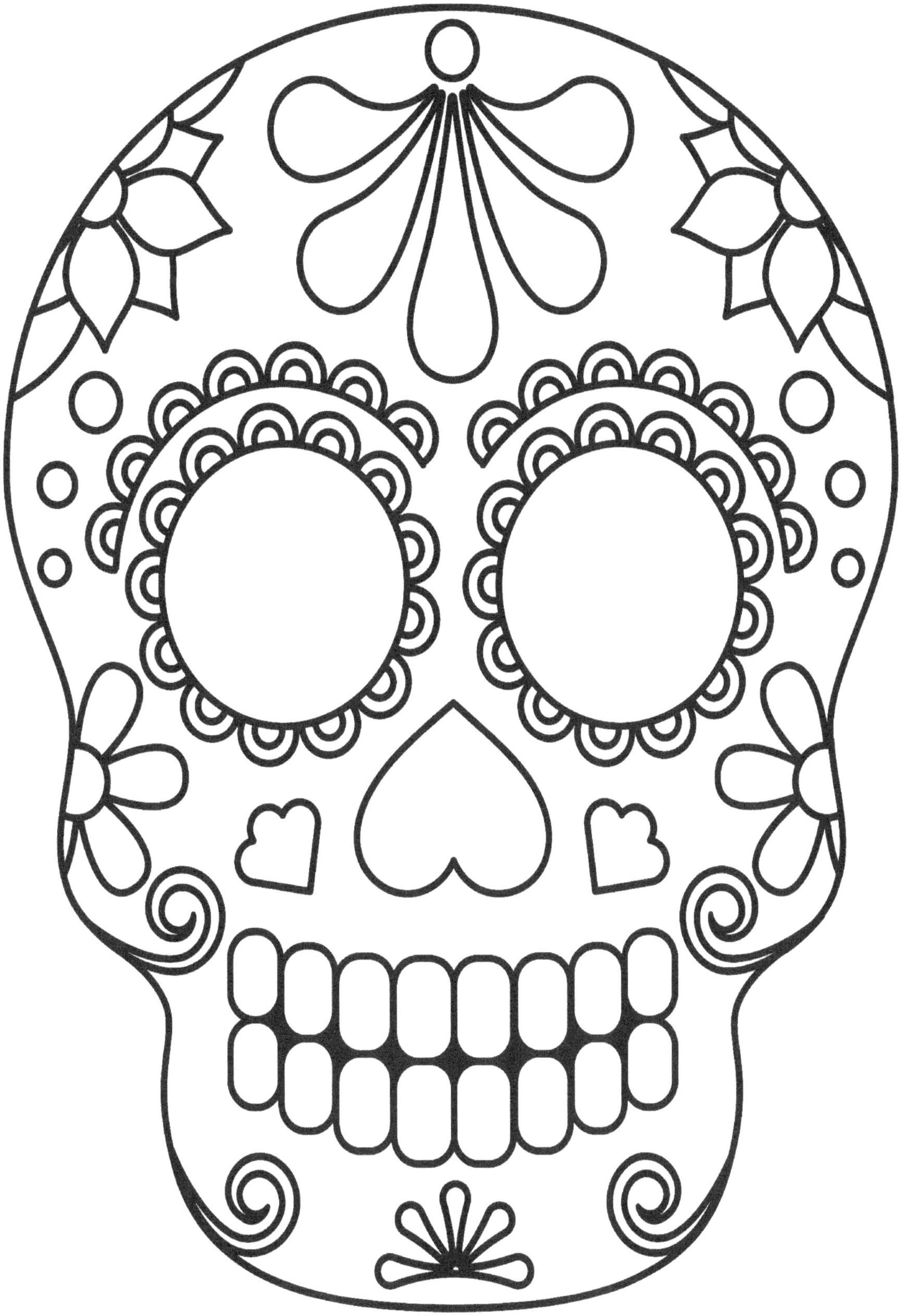

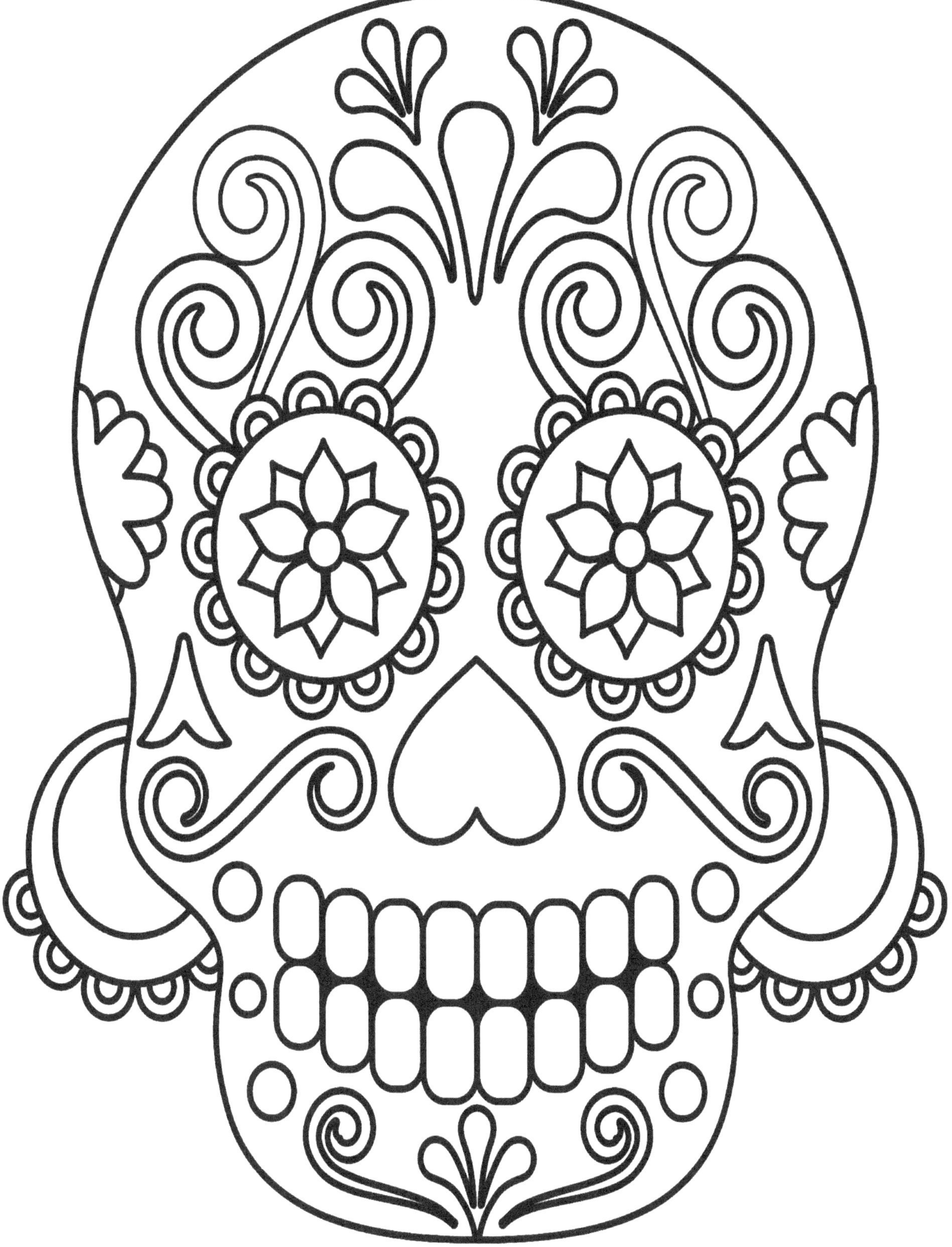

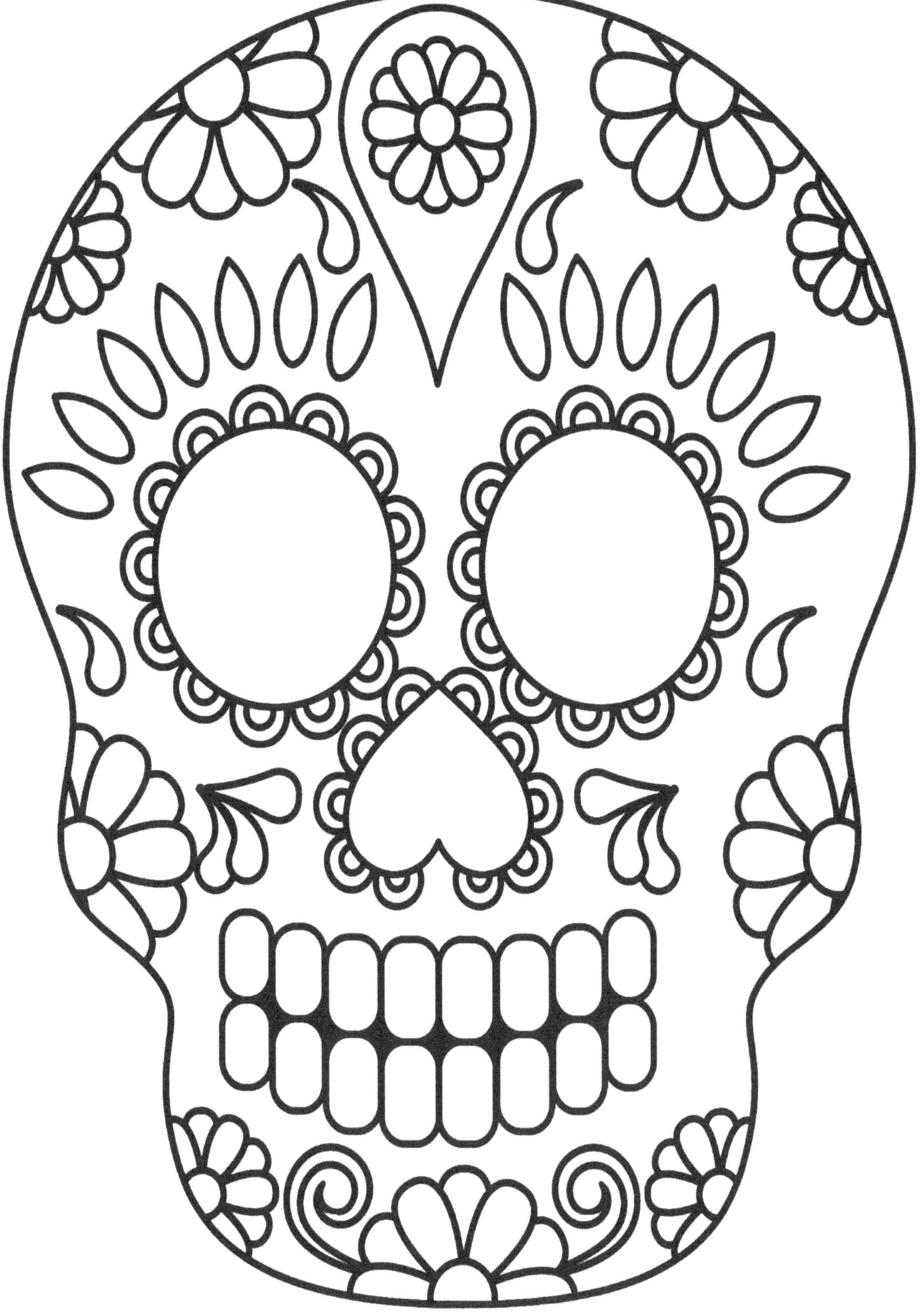

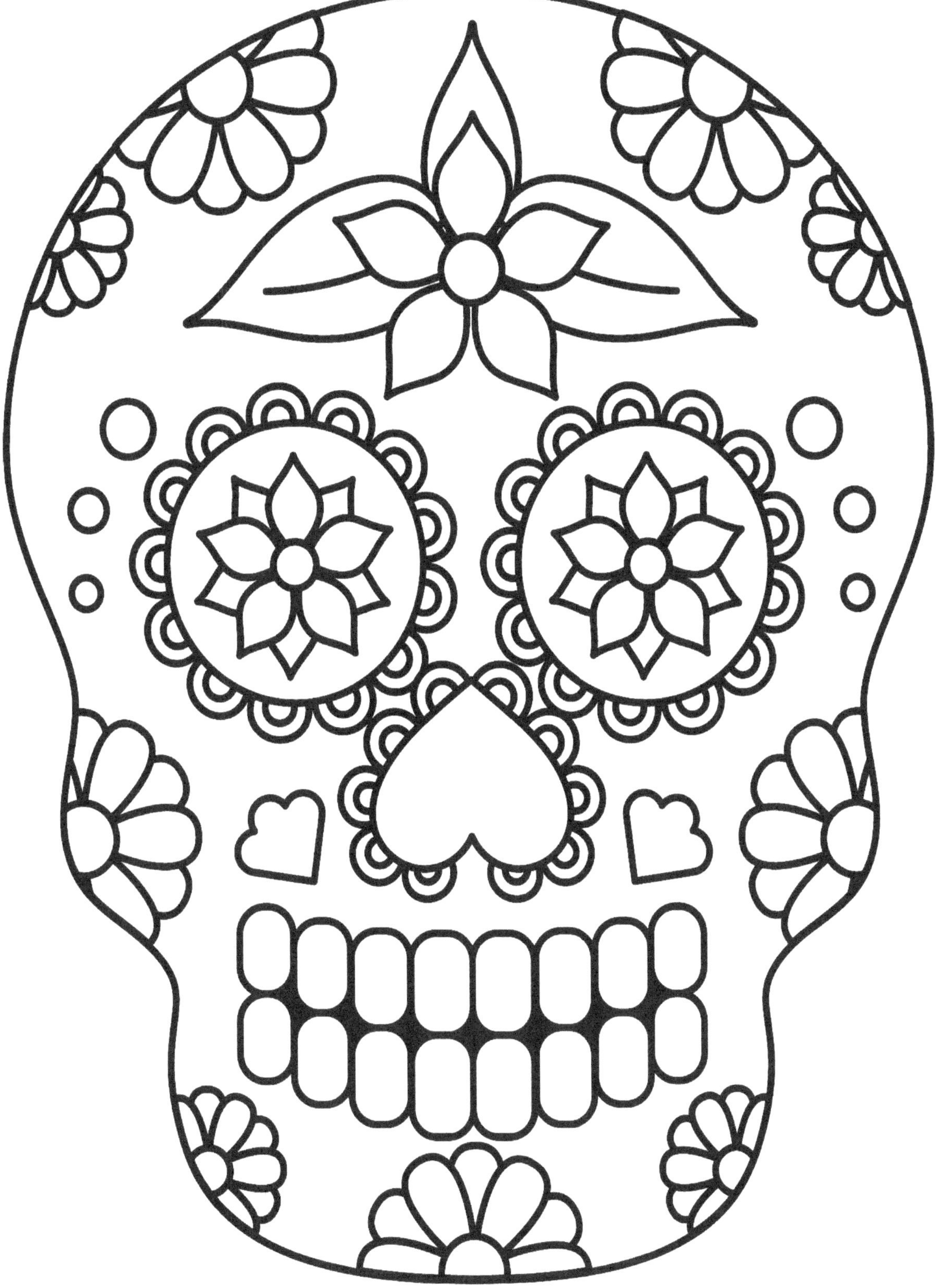

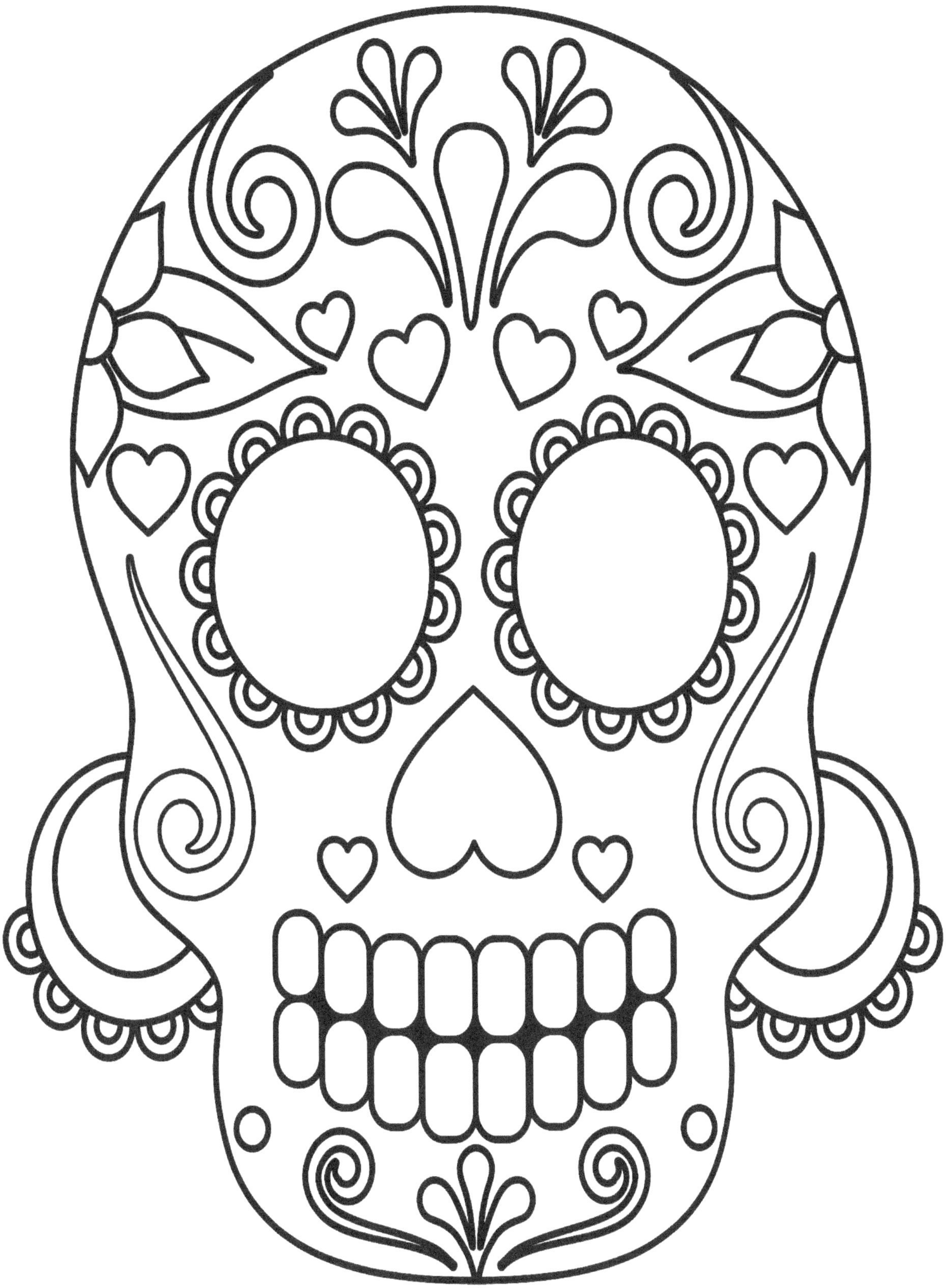

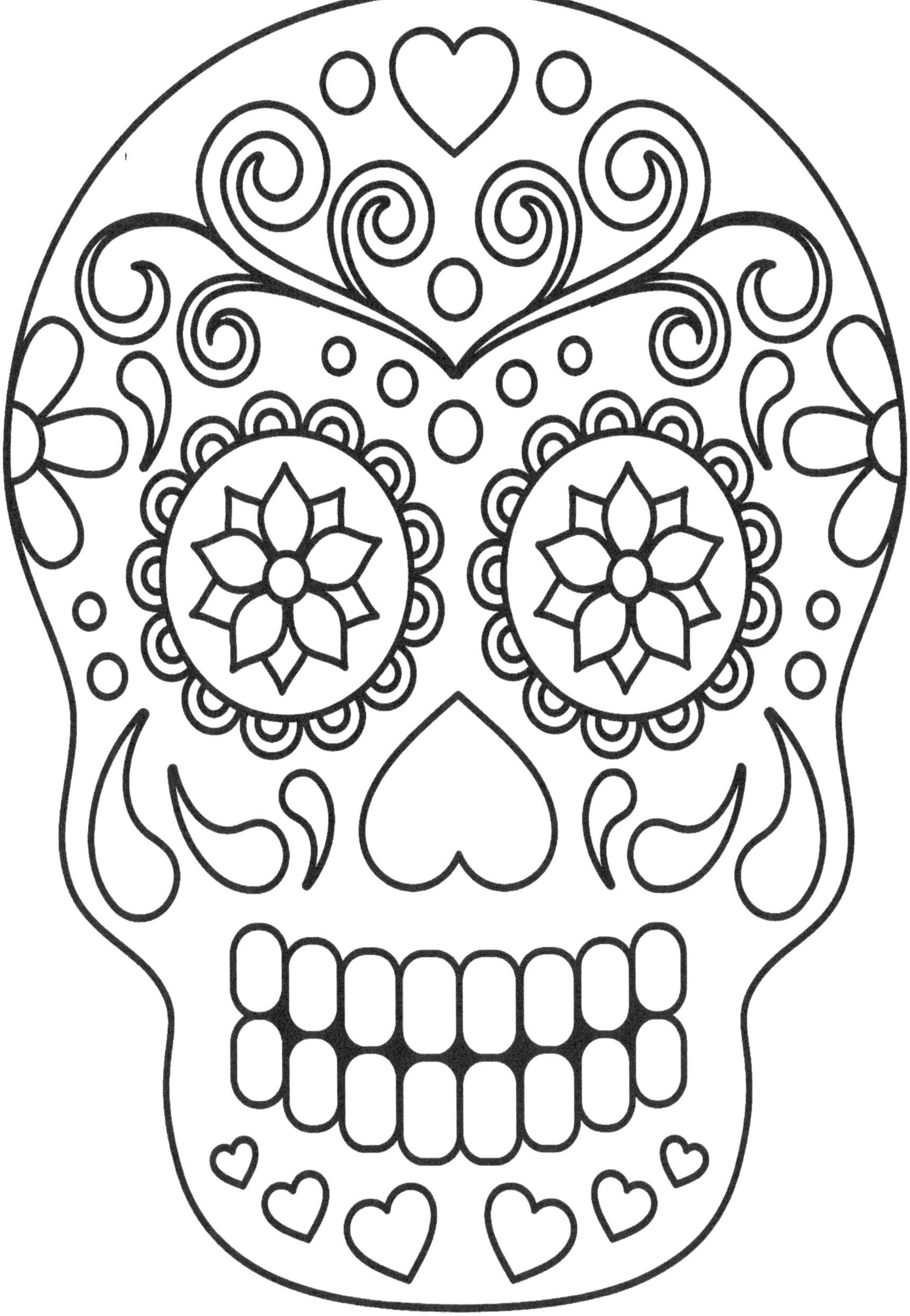

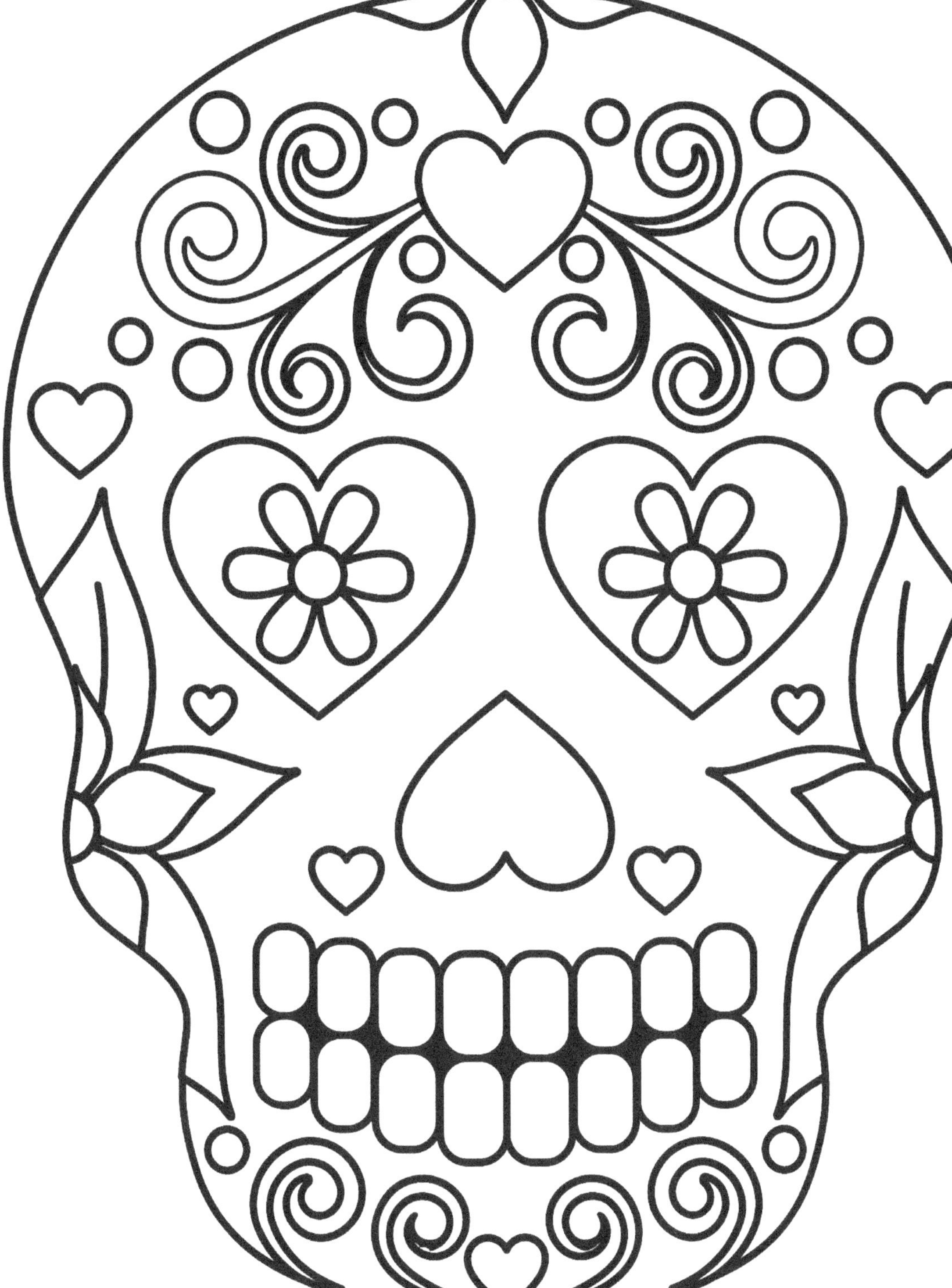

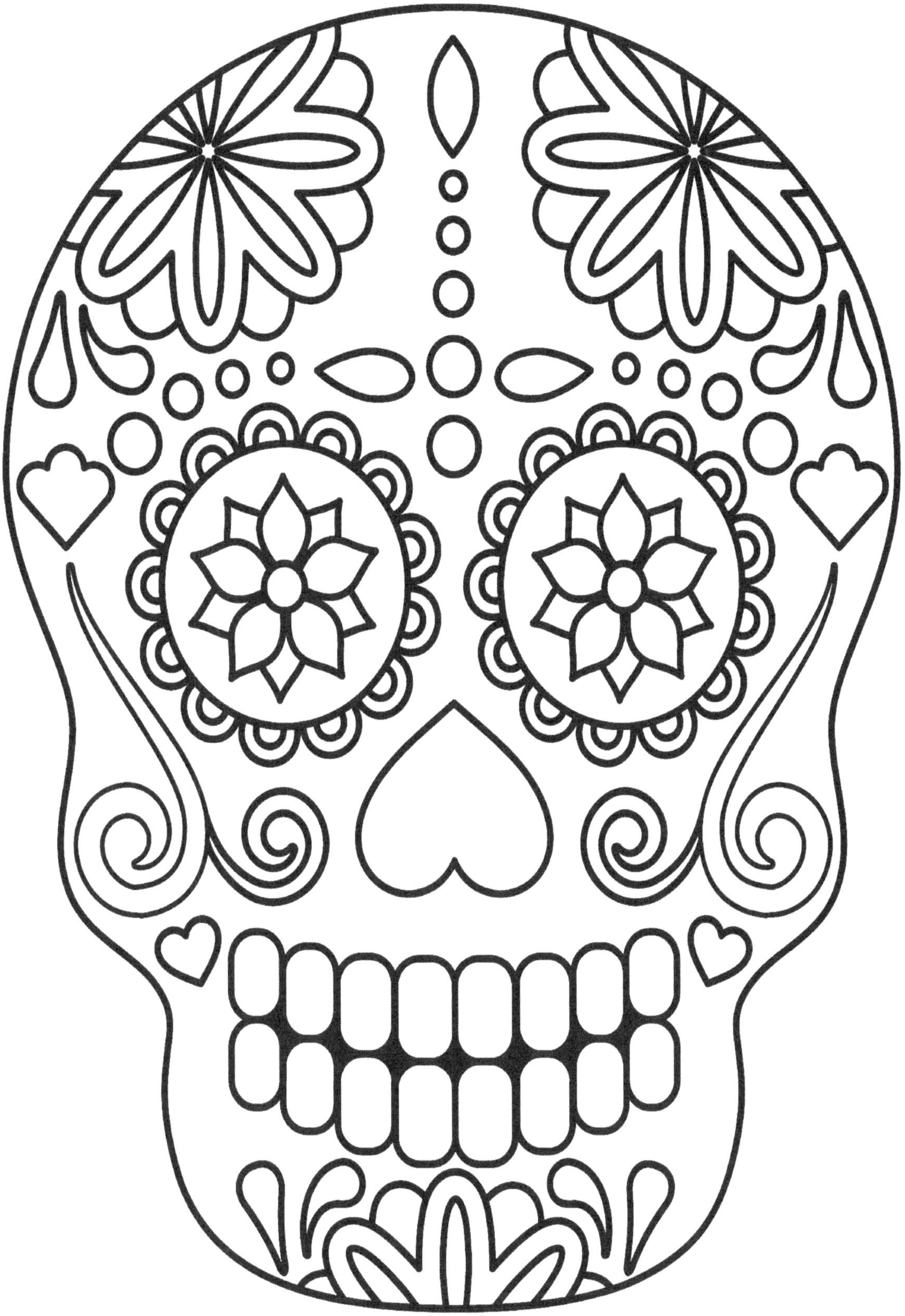

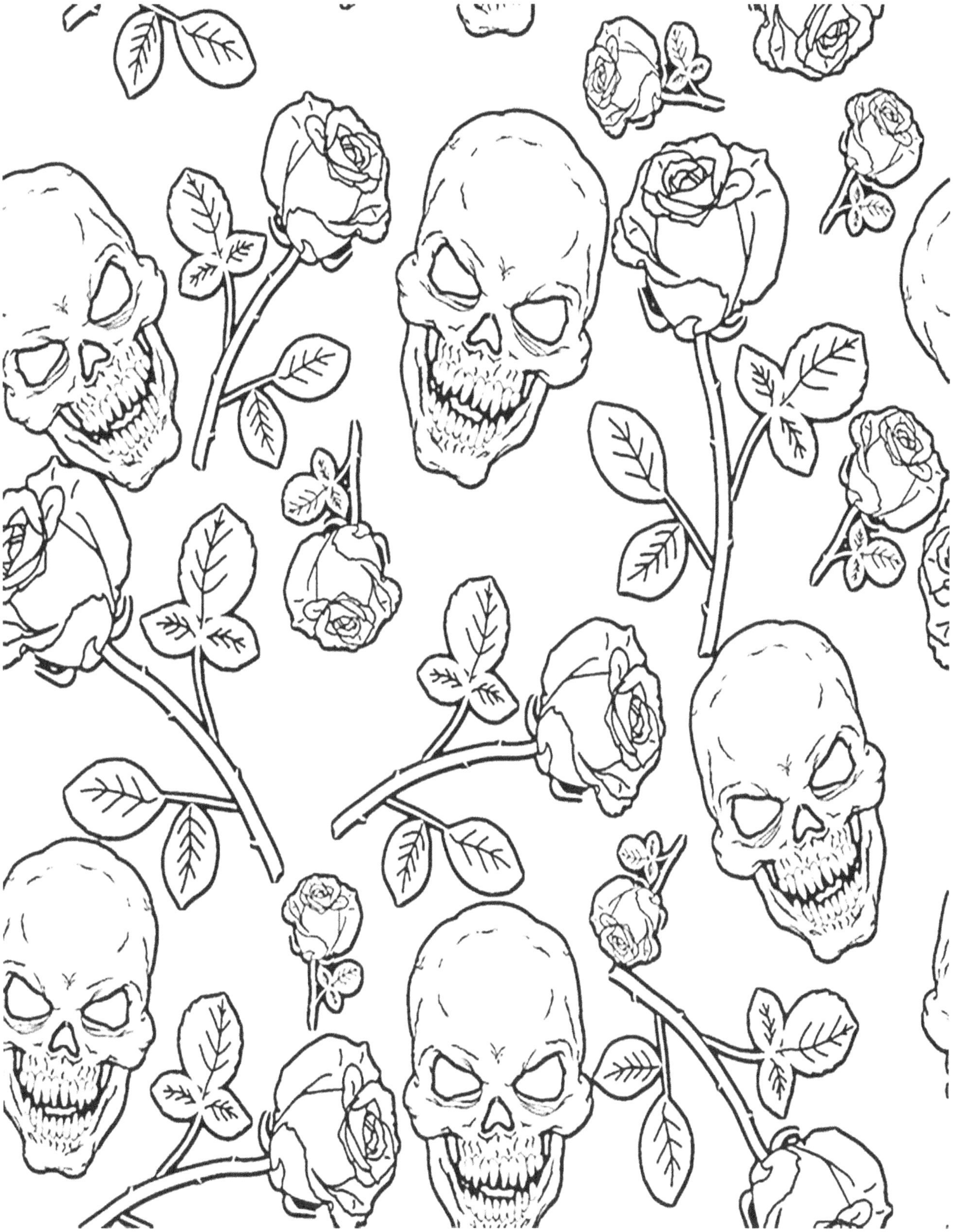

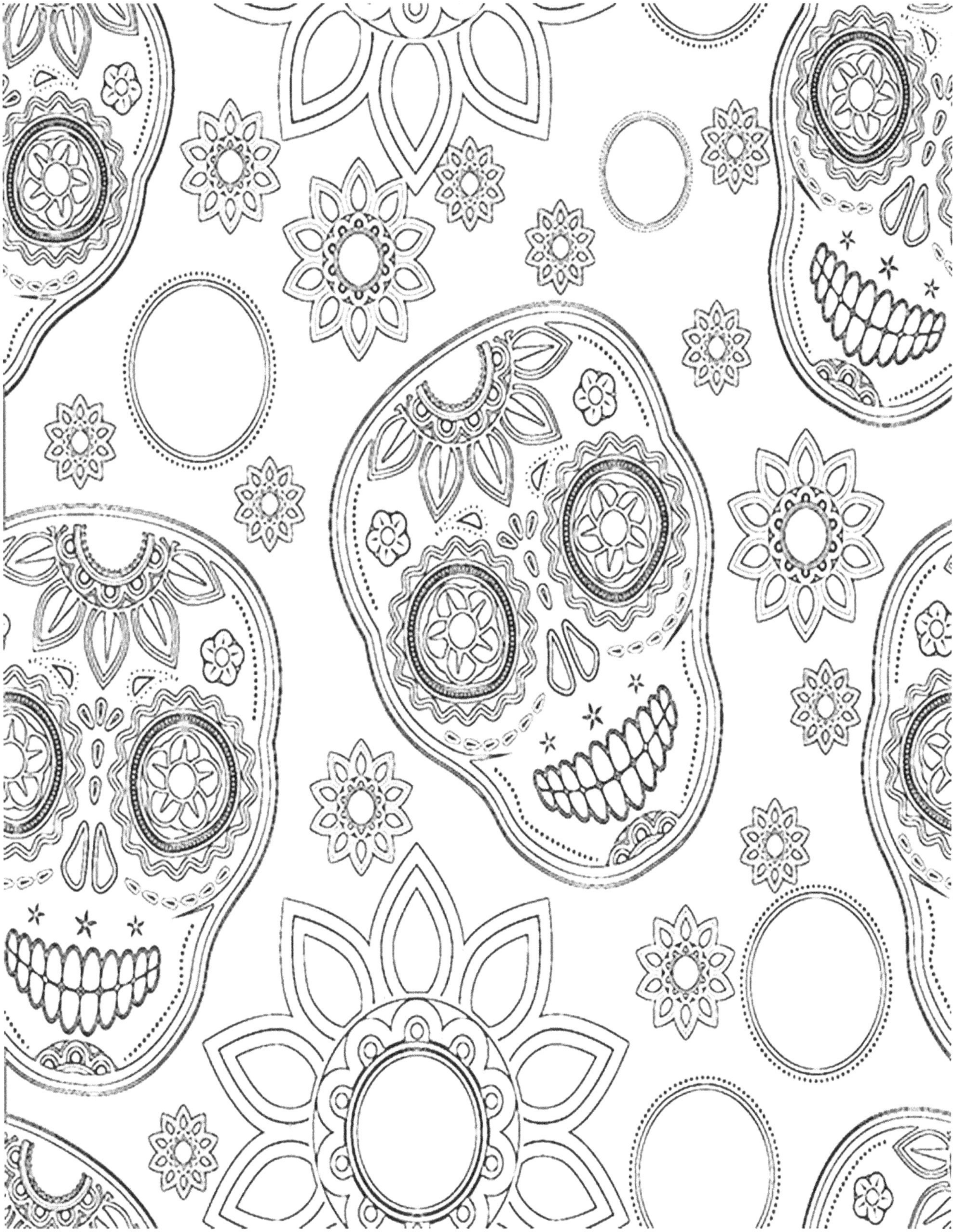

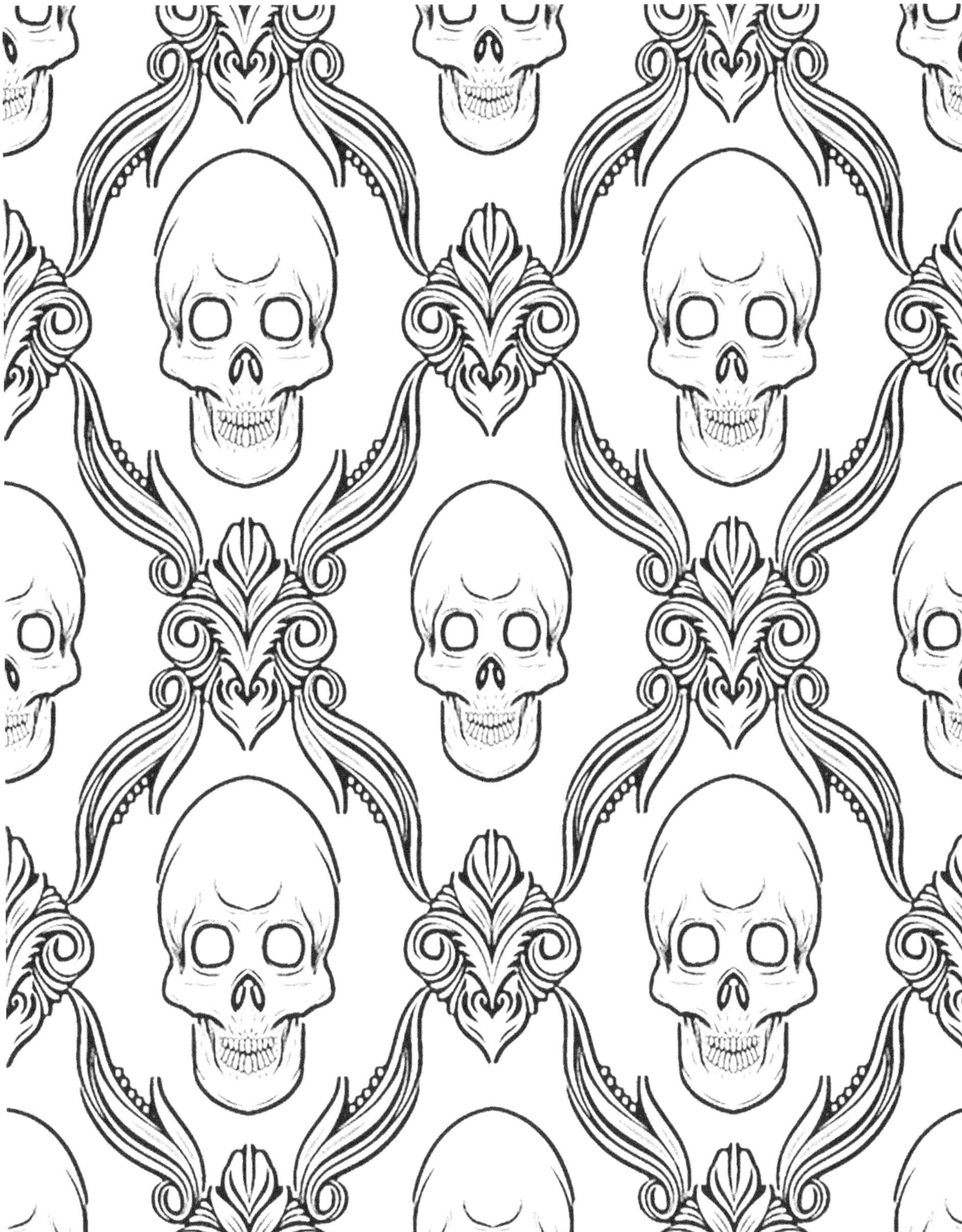

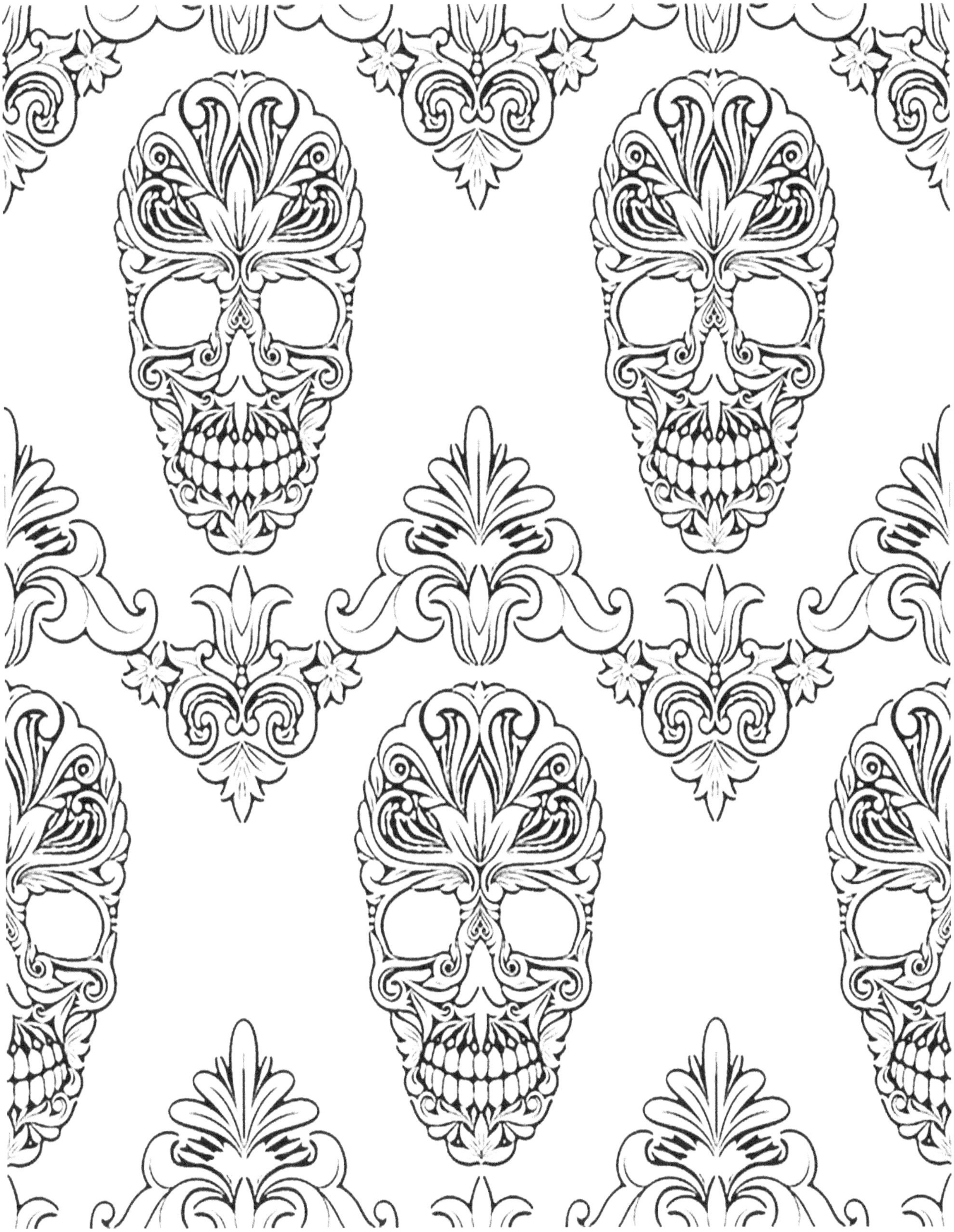

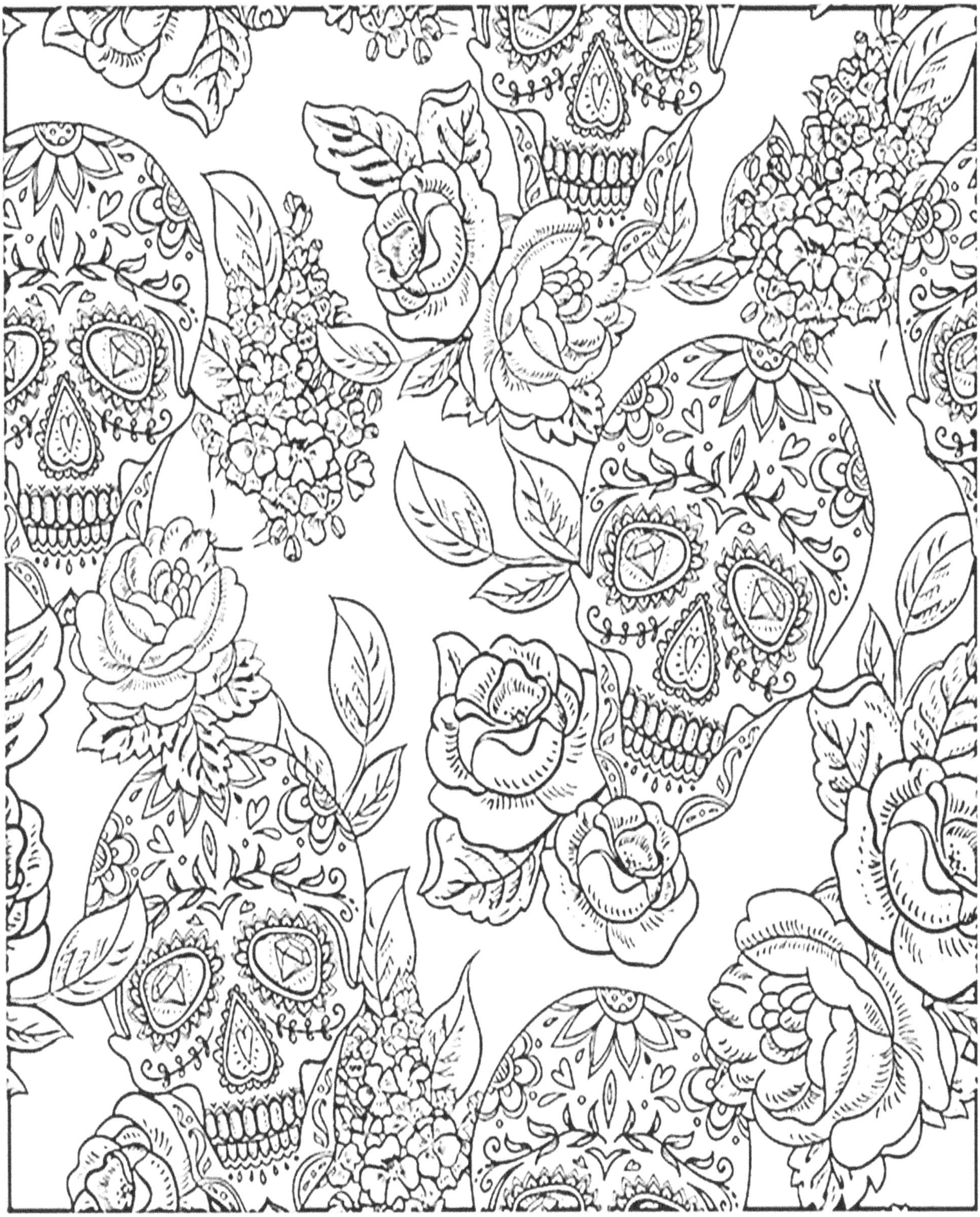

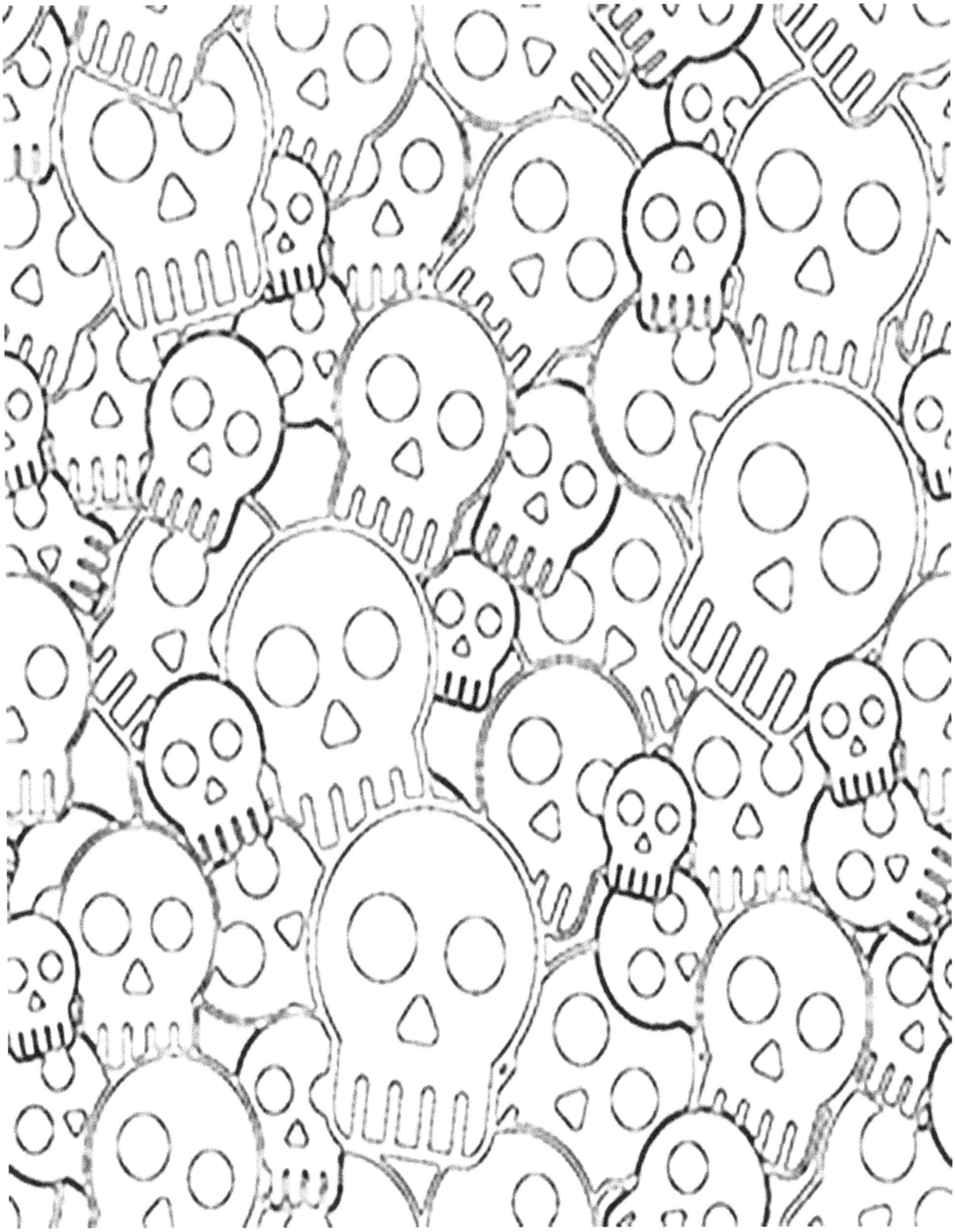

www.ingramcontent.com/pod-product-compliance
Lightning Source LLC
Chambersburg PA
CBHW080647180526
45168CB00008B/3332
* 9 7 8 1 5 1 7 2 6 1 9 1 7 *